AUGUST VON KOTZEBUE: THE COMEDY, THE MAN

By the Same Author

1961. *A Definition of Tragedy*. Reprint: 1982.
1963. *The Theatre of Don Juan: A Collection of Plays and Views, 1630-1963.*
1964. *Chi Po and the Sorcerer: A Chinese Tale for Children and Philosophers.*
1967. *The Fatal French Dentist*: a play.
1967. *The Gobble-Up Stories*: fables.
1968. *Seven Comedies by Marivaux*: translations, critical introduction. Reprint: 1984.
1970. *Five Comedies of Medieval France*: translations, critical introduction. Reprint: 1982.
1970-72. *Collected Plays*: original drama in two volumes.
1971. *Three Classic Don Juan Plays*: based on the 1963 volume.
1974. *Simplicities*: poems.
1976. *The Patriots of Nantucket: A Romantic Comedy of the American Revolution.*
1976. *Amphitryon*: an adaptation of Molière's comedy.
1978. *The Land of Upside Down*: translated from Ludwig Tieck's *Die verkehrte Welt*, with critical introduction.
1981. *Annotations to 'Vanity Fair'*. Second edition, with John Sutherland: 1988.
1981. *Collected Lyrics and Epigrams.*
1981. *Philoctetes and the Fall of Troy: Plays, Documents, Iconography, Interpretations.*
1982. *Ariadne*: translated from the *Ariane* of Thomas Corneille, and followed by an essay, "*Ariadne* and Neo-Classical French Tragedy."
1985. *The Book of Elaborations*: essays.
1987. *The Kukkurik Fables.*
1988. *Sigismund, Prince of Poland: A Baroque Entertainment*: a play.

AUGUST VON KOTZEBUE: THE COMEDY, THE MAN

Including
The Good Citizens of Piffelheim,
translated from
Die deutschen Kleinstädter

Oscar Mandel

The Pennsylvania State University Press
University Park and London

Library of Congress Cataloging-in-Publication Data

Mandel, Oscar.
    August von Kotzebue : the comedy, the man.

    Bibliography: p.
    Includes index.
    1. Kotzebue, August von, 1761-1819. 2. Authors,
German—18th century—Biography. I. Kotzebue, August
von, 1761-1819. Deutschen Kleinstadter. English. 1989.
II. Title
PT2387.Z5M36 1989   832'.6   88-43438
ISBN 0-271-00668-4

Copyright © 1990 The Pennsylvania State University

Printed in the United States of America

CONTENTS

Preface

The double purpose of this book is to dust off, for the English-speaking public, the fascinating yet all but forgotten figure of August von Kotzebue (1761-1819), one of those many men and women of talent and genius who turned little Weimar unexpectedly into a capital of intellectual Europe in the age of Goethe and Schiller; and to offer the first translation into English ever made of Kotzebue's acknowledged masterpiece, *Die deutschen Kleinstädter*—literally *The Small-Town Germans* but here baptized as *The Good Citizens of Piffelheim*. In my commentary upon this comedy I will propose the thesis that *Die deutschen Kleinstädter* is the final valuable text in the long European series of what are conveniently called neoclassical comedies.

During his own lifetime and for a solid generation thereafter, Kotzebue's plays dominated the theaters of Europe and America. He was bread and butter to managers in dozens of countries. Some forty of his plays—give or take a few—were translated into English alone, several of them more than once, and printed and reprinted on both sides of the Atlantic. It may surprise, therefore, that the work I have just called his acknowledged masterpiece should have remained unknown in our language, manifesting itself in England only in the original German as two school-editions, dated 1857 and 1884. As will be seen by and by, Kotzebue's reputation—especially outside the German-speaking world—rested chiefly on his larmoyant and melodramatic pieces. In Germany itself, *Die deutschen Kleinstädter* had been well received in its day but without the fanfare that would have drawn particular attention abroad. By the time those who cared realized that Kotzebue's best work had been comic, and that his satire on the German petty bourgeoisie was his best comedy, it was too late: Kotzebue was "out," and anything of his left untranslated by chance was condemned to remain so, perhaps forever.

A few years ago, when I published my translation of Ludwig Tieck's *Die verkehrte Welt* (*The Land of Upside Down*)—a bizarre comedy nearly contemporaneous with Kotzebue's and equally unknown in the English-speaking world—I alluded briefly to the enmity between Tieck and Kotzebue. The first was an ardent Romantic, given to unearthly flights of the imagination, and addressing his work to an intellectual elite. The second was a down-to-earth left-over from the Enlightenment, a sentimentalist, and a roaring commercial success. I imagine that neither man would have relished the idea of sharing the same translator, except as a bad joke. And yet a sound moral can be drawn from this joke, to wit, that the history of the arts is replete with wasted battles. Every new school proclaims a revolution and decrees oblivion or damnation against its opponents and predecessors. Fifty or a hundred years later, a fresh generation, busy with its own absurd quarrels, realizes that former quarrels were absurd; that either/or was a delusion; that the fur did not need to fly. It turns out, for instance, that Romanticism and Classicism are both precious. Or, as Walter Pater phrased it in his essay on Romanticism, "In that *House Beautiful* which the creative minds of all generations . . . are always building together for the refreshment of the human spirit, these oppositions cease." And so it befalls that the translator of an ultra-Romantic comedy by Tieck applies himself with equal pleasure and intellectual profit to an ultra-Classical comedy by Kotzebue, just as a museum curator blithely hangs in the same room Fragonard and David, Ingres and Delacroix. Our retroactive wisdom—seldom enforced on the present— instructs us that if the two poles existed, they existed because mankind wanted them both.

With regard to the critical, historical, and biographical half of this volume, I feel that its length and minuteness are justified intrinsically by the decided power to interest of the subject itself, and extrinsically by the absence in the English language of any comparable study. In the second half, consisting of the annotated translation, I have made an effort to accommodate both the academician and the professional theater-person. In order to present a usable script for immediate staging—and Kotzebue's comedy is a "natural" for the stage here and now—I have taken the liberty of retouching a few passages which would puzzle audiences today, without in any way creating what is called an adaptation. For instance, when a character, in the original, offers to write an Ode to the *Mumme* of Braunschweig (a kind of beer), surely no violence is done to Kotzebue by substituting, for our own audiences, Piffelheim beer. In context, this remains in full accord with the intended spirit of the German text. Such then are the scope and nature of my tampering with Kotzebue. On the other hand, the student and scholar must have Kotzebue's precise allusions, *Mumme* and all. These they will find faithfully translated and explained in the notes. The latter also enable an unusually reverent director to mount a production conforming as closely as he wishes to Kotzebue's exact topicalities.

I am happy to offer my thanks to Maria Kelsen Feder, who, after helping me with Tieck and, afterwards, with my translation of Heiner Müller's *Philoktet*, again read the entire manuscript and corrected a number of slips. I also extend my thanks to the Deutscher Akademischer Austauschdienst, whose summer grant in 1984 allowed me to track down and read a great number of forgotten plays by Kotzebue's forgotten contemporaries. For individual tips, I am grateful to my Caltech colleague Sigrid Washburn, to Sigrid Kupsch-Losereit in Heidelberg, and to Denise Gluck in Paris.

Portrait of Kotzebue.
In H. Döring, *August von Kotzebues Leben.* Weimar, 1830.

Portrait of Frederick William III before his accession to the throne of
Prussia; painted by Francois Gérard.
In Friedrich Wilhelm, Prinz von Preussen, ed., *Preussens Könige*.
Gütersloh and Vienna, 1971.

The Royal Theater in Berlin, inaugurated in 1802.
In C. Schäffer and C. Hartmann, *Die Königlichen Theater in Berlin*.
Berlin, 1886.

ON KOTZEBUE
(Weimar 1761 — Mannheim 1819)

1

The Comic Playwright

The opinions delivered by scholars who have made extended studies of August von Kotzebue's plays are not encouraging. I begin with a few of their animadversions in order the better to situate the special critical argument I will be advancing. Pride of place goes to Karl Goedeke and his article on Kotzebue in the vast canonical bibliography of German authors that bears his name: "From the artistic point of view, Kotzebue's theatrical works are worthless, one and all."[1] Charles Rabany, concluding his biography of Kotzebue, grants the latter "at least a few lines in a general history of his times," enough at any rate, to justify "giving his biography a length which might be thought exaggerated."[2] Karl-Heinz Klingenberg berates Kotzebue's comedies for failing to raise the public's class-consciousness, and their author for having limited himself to "distracting, irrelevant entertainment."[3] For Otto Mann, "Kotzebue was firmly and one-sidedly gifted for comedy; however, he did not attempt to place his own stamp on it on a responsible level, but remained content with quick, clever, indeed virtuoso entertainment pieces."[4] Helmut de Boor and Richard Newald, after berating the playwright for his "unscrupulous" use of sources, conclude that he was incapable of "striving for a higher art."[5] Gerhard Giesemann, writing his authoritative history of Kotzebue's standing in Russia, confesses that "this inquiry concerns a 'third-rate' writer, all but forgotten today, although from the point of view of literary history his works are of the highest importance."[6] In a volume of even larger scope concerning Kotzebue and his times, Frithjof Stock early on disclaims any attempt to raise our estimation of Kotzebue: "To 'save' him is impossible. . . . He is worth a little more than his reputation allows, but when a reputation is as low as his, that is not saying much."[7] And finally Benno von Wiese: "Why is it worth our while to renew our access to Kotzebue's works? Clearly the reasons pertain rather to sociology than to aesthetics."[8]

These are not citations tendentiously lifted from a mixed bag of opinions. They represent a verdict few have challenged; indeed they perpetuate hostile judgments which far outweighed friendly commentary even in the years when

[1] Goedeke 1893, p. 272. [2] Rabany 1893, p. 143. [3] Klingenberg 1962, p. 156. [4] Mann 1963, p. 315.
[5] De Boor and Newald 1967, p. 394.   [6] Giesemann 1971, p. 15.   [7] Stock 1971, p. 9.
[8] In Mathes 1972, p. 13.

Kotzebue's plays—chiefly his melodramas—filled the world's theaters, that is to say during his entire active lifetime and for decades after his death. Critical antipathy—sometimes qualified by a few complimentary words about his comic gifts—simply persisted, and it is taken for granted today that Kotzebue is unsalvageable. As a playwright of staggering popularity from London to the Aleutians, going either eastward or westward, and as a man who left his mark on the political history of Germany (as we shall see), he necessarily remains a "phenomenon." The question is, can anything be done for him, at this late date, in the arena of pure aesthetics?

The affirmative answer I propose depends on a critical operation of drastic disentanglement which no one has thought of performing: picking one title, with perhaps a very few consorts, from a dense and obscuring mass. To use another metaphor, I wish to create a separate space for *Die deutschen Kleinstädter* (literally "The Small-Town Germans" but here translated as *The Good Citizens of Piffelheim*) away from the 230-odd plays by Kotzebue which all but smother it. The election of *Die deutschen Kleinstädter* for this separate space is not arbitrary. Critics unanimously see it—condescendingly enough—as Kotzebue's best work, and it enjoys the unique distinction of being currently in print in three editions. That is encouragement enough for a bold next step, namely to assert that this modest comedy, without regard to the merits or defects of anything else Kotzebue ever wrote, has every right, aesthetically speaking, to cohabit with such plays as Machiavelli's *Mandragola*, Lope de Vega's *La dama boba*, Molière's *L'Avare*, Vanbrugh's *The Relapse*, Marivaux's *Les fausses confidences*, Holberg's *Den politiske Kandstober*, Goldoni's *Le smanie della villegiatura*, Beaumarchais' *Le barbier de Séville*, and Sheridan's *The Rivals*.

These, and many others, form a fairly cohesive family of comic drama. The qualitative difference among them is moderate. Some readers will prefer one, some another; but there is no question here of a grand breakthrough for this one, or a calamitous failure for that one. By the same token, *Die deutschen Kleinstädter* is neither a prodigy in this company nor a poor relation. It is one of them. Or rather should be. And would have been (I am arguing) if the bad odor emanating from those 230-odd plays had not subtly affected the German critics' perception. They could praise *Die deutschen Kleinstädter*, but, unwittingly disheartened by those innumerable shoddy plays, they could not bring themselves to admire it as they would have if Kotzebue had written this and nothing else.

Other obstacles have stood in the way. One of them may be the overly strong sense, in German criticism, of the division between high and low literature. I do not know whether we need to invoke a national bent in favor of high seriousness and intellectual or moral elevation, but the fact is that German critics are too fond of the labels "trivial" and "entertaining." Once these labels are affixed to a text, it goes into a common mental cubbyhole where it is lost to Literature. Foreign trivia are exempt. Perhaps the prestige of being foreign gives them the lift needed to escape from the fatal cubbyhole. But for native works little quarter is given. As a result, a capital distinction—one which obviously affects our play—is effaced. For the history of the arts—of all the arts—demonstrates incontrovertibly that there are good trifles and bad trifles, trifles that prove perdurable for the very same elite which belittles them, and trifles that vanish with the morning dew. These critics do not reflect that there is one permanence for *Eroicas*, and another for *Serva padronas*. That masterpieces range from immensities to miniatures. That the human spirit requires both. That aesthetic success is equally difficult all along the line. That each ever so rare success at each level of seriousness is precious.

If this much is granted, it must still be admitted that Kotzebue himself made a light-fingered discrimination difficult. Goethe and Schiller left the throne of German comedy vacant, as Platen once remarked, but how could it occur to critics that meretricious Kotzebue might be placed on it? In his own time, he owed his "commercial" triumphs chiefly, as I have said, to a stream of melodramatic and sentimental dramas—beginning with his world-famous *Menschenhass und Reue* (Misanthropy and Remorse, 1788). Its concluding episode will suffice to show us Kotzebue as his contemporaries saw him. The story concerns a very young wife, seduced in a heedless moment three years before, who fled the husband and children she still loved to expiate her sin in humble, anonymous service on a noble estate, while her disconsolate husband, the Baron Meinau—now turned into The Stranger—became a mankind-hating recluse. Since by Kotzebuan chance his hermitage and the noble estate are in the same vicinity, husband and wife have come face to face again. We join them outdoors at the end of the play, in a scene which galvanized spectators all over Europe and America.

EULALIA. O generous man! I implore you, allow me to see my children again ere we part, that I may press them against my heart, that I may bless them, that I may kiss their father's features in their own.
THE STRANGER *remains silent.*
EULALIA (*after a pause*). Ah! If you knew how I longed for my children during these three dreadful years; how my tears would fall whenever I saw a boy or a girl of the same age; how I would sit sometimes at dusk in my lonely room, feeding on the magical images my lively fantasy aroused, now of Wilhelm, now of Malchen, cradled in my lap—O! Do allow me to see them one more time! But *one* motherly embrace! And then we part forever.
THE STRANGER. Willingly, Eulalia—this very evening—I expect the children at any moment—they were brought up in the little town nearby—thither I sent my servant—he may have returned by this time—I give you my word, as soon as they come, I shall send them to the house. They may, if you wish, remain with you till dawn tomorrow—then I shall take them back again—(*Pause*)

(This interview has been overheard "with the deepest emotion" by Eulalia's noble friends and employers. The children have in fact arrived. As it is dark, the friends have been able to secrete the boy behind the mother and the girl behind the father. They are in effect staging a drama within the drama).

EULALIA. So we shall have nothing more to say to each other in this life. (*Collecting all her resolve*) Farewell, noble man! (*She presses his hand into hers*) Forget an unhappy woman who will never forget you! (*She kneels*) Allow me to press my lips to this hand one more time; this hand, which once was mine!
THE STRANGER (*raising her*). No abasement, Eulalia! (*He shakes her hand*). Farewell!
EULALIA. Farewell!
THE STRANGER. Farewell!
EULALIA. We part without anger—
THE STRANGER. Without anger.
EULALIA. And when at last I have expiated long enough; when we meet again in a better world—
THE STRANGER. There, prejudices hold no sway; and then you can be mine again!
(*They are still holding hands; their eyes sadly meet. They stammer another "Farewell!" and part; but as they move away, Eulalia discovers little Wilhelm, and Meinau sees Malchen*)
MALCHEN. Father—
WILHELM. Mother—
(*Father and mother wordlessly embrace the children*)
MALCHEN. Dear father—
WILHELM. Dear mother—
(*Father and mother tear themselves away from the children, look at one another, spread their arms wide, and rush into each other's arms*)
THE STRANGER. I forgive you!
(*The Countess and the Major lift the children, who cling to their parents, crying "Dear father, dear mother."*)

THE END[9]

This sensationally influential scene characterizes—I repeat—the Kotzebue the world knew. A chapter might be written about nearly every line of dialogue,

[9] My translation. In England, the play was translated as *The Stranger, or, Misanthropy and Repentance,* and went through many editions and printings from 1798 on.

every stage direction, and even the punctuation; and one can begin to understand, what with "There, no prejudices rule" and Meinau's readiness to melt, why critics sobbed their hearts out—and accused Kotzebue of making immorality attractive. A few might have noted that the play contains some excellent comic scenes. But the point I am making here is that, after scores of such plays, and almost each one of them a hit—plays in which Kotzebue moralized and philosophized and sentimentalized,[10] plays replete with chance and coincidence, unlikely reversals, easy magnanimities and melting reconciliations, it became far more difficult for criticism to extract and isolate a work like *Die deutschen Kleinstädter* than to save Molière and Sheridan from their single ventures into tragedy.[11] It was easy to disentangle Congreve from his one and only *Mourning Bride*, difficult to lift *Die deutschen Kleinstädter* from a magma of *Poverty and Nobleness of Mind, The Wanderer or the Rights of Hospitality, False Shame, Count Benyowsky or the Kamtchatka Conspiracy, The Negro Slaves*, and so on and on. For ten fateful years—between *Menschenhass* and *Die beiden Klingsberg*—Kotzebue, not yet fully aware of his talent for comedy, had filled European theaters and made himself famous with his serious drama. When A. W. Schlegel attacked him, in 1800, in a book-full of satirical pieces, it never occurred to him even to mention the two or three comic plays Kotzebue had produced by that time. Kotzebue had made his bed, so to speak, and had to lie in it: he was the man for tears and shudders. So he was for Madame de Staël much later when she wrote of him with a mixture of respect and censure (she had doubts, like most people, about the morality of his soul-wrenching dramas)[12] —and so he remained, still later, for Carlyle:

[10] While the judgment of what does or does not constitute a remote coincidence is unlikely to vary greatly from one epoch to another, the same cannot be said of men's notions of what is and what is not an improbable act of charity, forgiveness, self-sacrifice, reconciliation and so forth. This means that the verdict of sentimentality is apt to vary not only from epoch to epoch (as a whole), but also, in any given epoch, from person to person. Now it is true that some of the more intelligent readers and spectators of Kotzebue's time were fully cognisant of, and repelled by, his outrageous sentimentalities, that is to say his unscrupulous assaults on probability with respect to benevolent emotions and actions. But to a surprising extent, the European and American elite "swallowed" fictions which make our own elite snicker. In my opinion, this difference is due to the far greater optimism concerning the realities—the non-textual realities in the non-fictive world—of our character, behavior and destiny which prevailed during the stretch of time we call the Enlightenment and Romanticism. One effect of such optimism would be to shift "upward" the public's evaluations of probability in works of art as compared with out own estimates. A sweet scene in a novel, a play, or a painting which we dismiss as highly improbable or downright impossible in the non-fictive world and therefore sentimental as literature or painting, our forefathers would often deem possible and even probable in the real world and therefore legitimately touching in a work of art. A simpler way of stating essentially the same thing is that our ancestors were less cynical than we are, and therefore both created and innocently enjoyed creations by others which we too disabused to accept. Remains the question whether they were or we are more in the right concerning mankind.
[11] Sheridan's highly successful *Pizarro* (1799) was in fact an adaptation of Kotzebue's *Spanier in Peru.*
[12] Staël 1814, Part II, chapter 25. In Part I, chapter 14, she briefly mentions *Die deutschen Kleinstädter*, but only to illustrate how proud every German is of the little place he inhabits. The French edition as we know it appeared in 1813.

Ill-fated Kotzebue, once the darling of theatrical Europe! . . . Were not these Plays translated into almost every language of articulate-speaking men; acted, at least, we may literally say, from Kamtschatka to Cadiz? Nay, did they not melt the most obdurate hearts in all countries, and . . . draw tears from iron cheeks? We ourselves have known the flintiest men, who professed to have wept over them, for the first time in their lives. . . .[13]

Indeed, the brand is on him to this day. A long article, signed by Benedikt Erenz, in a recent issue of *Die Zeit*, bears the title "Dallas 1788" and contemptuously names Kotzebue, *Menschenhass*, and his other *Rührstücke* (the German term, more dignified than ours, for tear-jerkers) as the ancestors of the television melodrama whose popularity is in fact Kotzebuish in its proportions.[14] No hint is dropped for the benefit of the journal's readers that Kotzebue had been the country's best comic playwright, almost its Goldoni.

So there is, in truth, a "Kotzebue case," and, I believe, nothing resembling it in the history of letters. But if the task of "precipitating" a single comical solid from the murk of so many once notorious Rührstücke is a difficult one, surely it need not daunt us. We have only to reaffirm the not very controversial aesthetic law that the company does not contaminate the individual. A text is a text, a score is a score, a painting is a painting. The strength of a given work is neither increased because the artist has created a hundred other strong works, nor diminished because his other hundred works are weak. *The artist* is indeed raised or lowered accordingly in our eyes; but the single work of art is not—or rather should not be: for here we return to the subconscious proclivity. It is hard not to be demoralized by the press of two hundred weak texts; hard not to inflict, without quite knowing it, guilt by association. But as soon as we become conscious of the psychological trap, it is easily avoided. The critical mind shakes off the bad company and readily gives Kotzebue the same chance it would offer him had he written no other play in his entire life than *Die deutschen Kleinstädter*. Until we find other texts worth saving, we must treat him as we do the author of *Lazarillo de Tormes*, or the Benjamin Constant of *Adolphe*: men of single productions, without before or after.

Say then that we have mentally disentangled Kotzebue from his serious plays. Say moreover that we have overturned a condemnation of his comedies and farces based on philosophic "triviality" or failure to anticipate Marx. Another difficulty then remains, once more created by Kotzebue himself. "He is one of those writers," observed J. G. Seume, "of whom it may be said that they would have written more had they written less—had they concentrated their especial gift so as to perfect a few individual works."[15] Kotzebue, alas, wrote not only

[13] Carlyle 1888, I, pp. 271-272. The quotation is from his "German Playwrights," published in 1829, ten years after Kotzebue's death.
[14] Erenz 1985, pp. 49-50.
[15] In W. von Kotzebue 1881, p. 88.

too many "elevated" plays; he also flooded the market, after the turn of the century, with too many funny ones. Like Lope de Vega, with whom he is often compared, he remained indefatigable long after he had lost any need to fatigue himself, whether for money or for glory. Revisiting a multitude of comedies, farces, vaudevilles, parodies, and operettas (I do not pretend to have read them all), the conscientious critic who has already eliminated the Elevated Drama must proceed to apply the sieve to the comic products.

Many of these are so trivially trivial (if one may so put it) that nothing should be said of them whatever; Kotzebue himself would surely have wanted them to be forgotten. Many contain charming episodes but fail to cohere as wholes. Most, like the serious plays, fall into sentimentality: they might have been delightful if Kotzebue had not acceded to the great public's penchant for tearful happiness based on utterly improbable exhibitions of human goodness.[16] Perhaps a small example will suffice. In *Die beiden Klingsberg* (The Two Klingsberg, 1799)—one of his best major comedies—we no sooner think that we shall be enjoying a tough, cynical trifle worthy of British Restoration or French Regency comedy than the elderly rake, Count Klingsberg, is caught doubling the pension of some poor children recently orphaned of their widowed mother. At the news, his valet "wipes a tear from his eye"—one of Kotzebue's favorite stage-directions. Let this instance speak for hundreds; and indeed for almost the whole standard repertory of German comedy after 1765, the date of Lessing's overrated *Minna von Barnhelm*.

Not only, then, does the critic have to rescue *Die deutschen Kleinstädter* from a mass of embarrassing serious plays; in order to create the space in which it can breathe, he must eliminate all or almost all of the comic ones as well. Such a wholesale clearing of the terrain would undoubtedly have surprised Kotzebue, and quite astonished him if presented as an attempt to restore his fame. He himself was of two minds regarding what would survive. Sometimes he was content to consider himself a public favorite not in the running against giants like Goethe and Schiller. "I know better than any critic," he wrote in his preface to *Der Graf von Burgund* (The Count of Burgundy, 1798) "that I do not write masterpieces, and that I am a playwright of the second rank. The chief aim of my plays is to be effective on stage; this goal they do achieve; and this is the point of view from which they ought to be judged."[17] Disclaimers of this sort are sprinkled among his works over a period of years. But the other Kotzebue felt that some of his works *were* in the running. Surely, he argued, so much success for so many years, so much applause in so many countries, and so many translations in print, proved that authentic quality did lodge somehow somewhere in

---

[16] The obverse needs to be stated as well: Kotzebue irrepressibly livened up many of his serious dramas with comic episodes which have retained their charm, isolated from the larmoyance surrounding them.

[17] Kotzebue 1840-1841, vol. 6.

many of his plays. "Illusion and fashion cannot persist that long."[18]

Perhaps his summation is the statement he composed in 1817 in an autobiographical piece he did not live to publish:

> I have written several hundred plays; therefore it should come as no surprise if, as is true for the even more numerous works of Lope de Vega, some of them are average or even downright bad. To begin with, then, I throw out a third, or at least a fourth of my plays. I wish I had not written them—at any rate not as they stand now; and if I should ever find a favorable hour to arrange for a collection of my dramatic works, I would not allow these rejected plays to appear, or else I would thoroughly rewrite them. But I suggest that if the rest escape condemnation, they will be enough to secure for me an honorable place among the dramatic writers of Germany.[19]

In other words, Kotzebue believed, or hoped, that his fame would be assured by at least a hundred and fifty of his plays, including, one may assume, a number of his weepy and shivery ones. In this he was obeying a perfectly normal expectation, for if a fertile artist has created one memorable work, surely, we all feel, he has produced several; surely he does not possess the capacity one day and lose it the next. But in fact Kotzebue did not lose it. He squandered it. His haste and his copiousness made him slovenly—*schluderhaft*, as Goethe remarked. The laws of probability notwithstanding, the more plays he wrote, the less was the likelihood of his producing good work; and he finally wrote so many that he reduced the probability to one, or very nearly one.

Another difficulty for Kotzebue in general, and *Die deutschen Kleinstädter* in particular, may well be that the man was, to put it baldly, a conservative in politics, even a reactionary, and one who flaunted his views. How, I wonder, would *Minna von Barnhelm*—the object of relentless idolatry to this day—be treated if Lessing had been on good terms with three tsars, a Habsburg emperor, and the Prussian royal family, as well as a mordant opponent of democracy, German national unity, liberal constitutional government, a free press, and student power? In Lessing's play all the sins for which Kotzebue is repudiated flourish: an excessively virtuous and declamatory hero, a melting scene in which he assures an impoverished widow that she does not owe him a pfennig, though she does and though he is sorely in need himself, another affecting episode in which a selfless servant refuses to abandon the master who cannot pay his wages, etc. *Minna* is idolized; the superior *Die deutschen Kleinstädter* barely survives at the margin. Might it have fared better if Kotzebue had died fighting for a democratic constitution? Over a century ago, the literary historian Rudolf Gottschall,

---

[18] Kotzebue 1814-1815, II, p. 186.
[19] Kotzebue 1821, pp. 29-30.

calling Kotzebue the German Molière, predicted that after the passing of nation-alistic literary historians [*burschenschaftlichen Literarhistoriker*], Kotzebue would receive his due at last.[20] But the prediction still awaits the event, and I believe that Kotzebue's politics continue to damage his reputation. I suspect that German critics do not want a classic, even a minor one, from such a man.

In a later section I will return to Kotzebue's life and politics. At this point, let me follow up on the hint I have dropped before, to the effect that *Die deutschen Kleinstädter* is not absolutely the only unblemished comedy Kotzebue ever wrote. I wanted to clear a space for it alone because, if I am not sharply mis-taken, only *Die deutschen Kleinstädter* has sufficient quality *and* magnitude (trifles too have magnitudes!) to join the European community of comedies I have named. But once this is done, I think we can surround his masterwork with a few comedies delightful enough to constitute a small *body* of memorable comic work; nothing like the hundred and fifty he foresaw, yet sufficient to give the author, in addition to the single work, the honorable place he spoke of, and that not only in German dramatic literature, but in the dramatic literature of Europe.

As can be guessed, anthologies of plays by Kotzebue have in fact appeared in the past—a number were published in his own lifetime and for as long as he was still "a name." But these collections reproduced what was famous, and therefore included some of Kotzebue's most turgid dramas, beginning always with his nemesis, *Menschenhass und Reue*. No attempt was ever made to perform the critical operation I have pleaded for. Instead, the consecrations perpetuated in the name of literary history prevented a fresh approach based uniquely on aesthetic considerations. It was always granted that Kotzebue had been at his best in comedy; but his comic work never manifested itself in its own critical or literal space, detached from the rest.

The one collection of his plays in print today, professor Jurg Mathes' selec-tion of *Schauspiele*, published in 1972, perpetuates the tangle. The editor—who is the foremost Kotzebue scholar of our time—would probably argue that in the absence of anything whatsoever in print by Kotzebue outside of *Die deutschen Kleinstädter*,[21] it made sense to bring out once more the works which literary history keeps naming, whatever their aesthetic merit. The anthology thus presents *Menschenhass und Reue, Die Indianer in England, Bruder Moritz der Sonderling* (Brother Moritz the Eccentric), *La Peyrouse, Die beiden Klingsberg, Die deutschen Kleinstädter*, and *Der Rehbock* (The Roebuck). Significantly, all of these plays except the last were written in the first half of Kotzebue's career, between 1788 and 1802. The first four "established" Kotzebue and are therefore essential to German literary history. The last three are invariably named as his

[20] Gottschall 1861, p. 204.

[21] I except two reprints: the account of his Siberian exile, *Das merkwürdigste Jahr meines Lebens* (München 1965); and his tract on the nobility, *Vom Adel* (Königstein/Ts 1978).

major comedies. But all these plays except *Die deutschen Kleinstädter* are either seriously or fatally marred by sentimentality, and four of them—the earlier ones—by Kotzebue's self-indulgent flood of "wise maxims" about life and love and mankind and what-have-you. The amount of *Kitsch* in them is awesome. Hence Benno von Wiese, who writes the introduction, has good reason for saying that the interest of such a book is chiefly historical: it reconstructs for us what was applauded in bygone times.

My imaginary alternate anthology proposes instead a "living" Kotzebue; a Kotzebue who wrote a handful of excellent comedies and farces, most of which never made literary or any other history. Unlike the Mathes anthology, it significantly displays *Die deutschen Kleinstäter* as the *earliest* of his viable comedies, and continues through the latter phase of Kotzebue's career, when he gave ever more of his time to comic writing. First after *Die deutschen Kleinstädter* comes *Incognito* (1804, v. 16),[22] a two-act drollery featuring Herr von Fuderkopf, who made a fortune in the Napoleonic wars selling wormy bread. Next we choose *Mädchenfreundschaft, oder der Türkische Gesandte* (Friendship Among Girls, or the Turkish Ambassador, 1805, v. 18), a one-act comedy in the spirit of *Cosi fan tutte*. Then another one-acter called *Die gefährliche Nachbarschaft* (Dangerous Neighbors, 1806, v. 19), much admired by Ludwig Börne, one of the very few contemporary intellectuals who gave a correct appraisal of Kotzebue's comic gifts. This is followed by *Der Kater und der Rosenstock* (The Cat and the Rose-Tree, 1807, v. 21) in the light verse which was one of Kotzebue's charming specialties. The sixth play is a rollicking parody of Goethe's *Stella* and Kotzebue's own *La Peyrouse*, namely *Der Graf von Gleichen* (Count von Gleichen, 1808, one act in verse, v. 21), rather spicy for its time. When the Count comes home from the Crusades with a Turkish princess in tow, both are cordially greeted by his German wife. He is looking forward to a happy threesome in bed; but the two wives start quarreling over dress, looks, and recipes; and all three grandly stab themselves to death in the end. Incidentally, this play was performed by courtly amateurs in Weimar in 1815—together with *Mädchenfreundschaft*. "Goethe, more imperious than ever . . . foamed and raged like a wounded boar," a foe of the great man—Karl August Böttiger—reported to Kotzebue, while Schiller's widow despaired at the low taste of the Weimar prince and the gentlemen who had frolicked about in this low farce. As for Kotzebue, Lotte Schiller wrote, "I have long since given up on him, and trust him ever to do the vile thing."[23]

---

[22] The volume numbers are those in the 1840-1841 edition of the plays. See the Bibliography.

[23] C. von Kotzebue 1911, pp. 88 and 90. The tale of the bigamous Count goes back to the 16th century and has received an astonishing number of treatments in German literature, both comic and tragic (see E. Frenzel, *Stoffe der Weltliteratur*, second edition, 1963). Still, in view of Kotzebue's very particular marital history, his predilection for the motif of the three-cornered marriage may have had something of a personal foundation.

In a number of his farces, Kotzebue contributed his mite to the hoary tradition of demystifying the Greek gods and goddesses. Solid authors stole these tales from the *commedia*, the *commedia* raided solid authors. The best of them in Kotzebue's opus is probably *Pandorens Büchse* (Pandora's Box, 1810, one act in verse, v. 24), in which he pours pepper over his favorite dishes: despotism and marriage. This, by the way, from a friend of monarchs and the loving husband of three wives (one after the other, I hasten to add): a God-given opportunity for a psychological dissection of the man! *Die Zerstreuten* (Absent-Minded Folk, 1810, v. 24) follows, with two Pantalone characters, one of whom pushes his son into the bedroom of the girl he would like for himself, while the other flirts with a young girl who is actually a boy in disguise: sexual ambiguities foreshadowing those which provoked an uproar when they appeared in the full-length *Rehbock*. As the ninth work I would offer the charming little *Blind geladen* (Loaded with Blanks, 1811, v. 25). Then *Die alten Liebschaften* (The Old Love Affairs, 1812, v. 27) a skit on a *Nozze di Figaro* motif; followed by *Das unsichtbare Mädchen* (The Invisible Girl, 1812, v. 27) a cynical little vaudeville in which Kotzebue once again mocks his own sentimentalities.

Besides his mythological farces, Kotzebue improvised a number of powder-puff Oriental tales, ready to be picked up by composers of operettas but standing firmly enough in their own pantoffles. Here too, of course, he was drawing upon and contributing to a venerable comic tradition. *Die Prinzessin von Cacambo* (1814, v. 30) is the one I would choose for our anthology. It concerns the conquest of a princess so beautiful that the very sight of her drives all men mad. Faithful to the tradition, Kotzebue uses these tales, along with a number of other fantasies (like *Die Brillen-Insel*, The Eyeglasses-Island, 1816) and several folk-comedies as so many quivers for his satirical barbs.

Our anthology might conclude with *Der Edukationsrath* (The Preceptor, 1816, v. 33), where a young rake disguised as a deceased pedagogue gives lessons to an aspiring libertine.[24]

In sum, for this innovative "Selected Comedies of August von Kotzebue" I propose *Die deutschen Kleinstädter* as the major play, with a merry dust of twelve satellites revolving around it. I reject a number of better known comedies like *Der Wildfang* (roughly The Young Scamp), *Der Wirrwarr* (Confusion) and *Pagenstreiche* (The Page's Pranks), all three too *schluderhaft* to be invited, and I have doubts concerning *Die beiden Klingsberg* and *Der Rehbock*[25] because of the sentimental patches which deface them. Both plays, it must be granted, offer scenes of high comedy and farce one is sorry to let go. If,

---

[24] Two of the little plays I have listed exist in English translations, unfortunately amateurish ones. They are *The Turkish Ambassador* and *The Old Love Affair*; both in *Seven One-Act Dramas*, translated by Beatrice B. Beebe [!] in *Poet Lore*, 38 (1927) 159-263.

[25] Under the title *Der Wildschütz*, *Der Rehbock* was turned into a charming opera by Albert Lortzing in 1842.

relenting, we admit them into our company, the result will be a two-volume anthology, still aimed at disentangling Kotzebue from his non-comic drama.

To characterize the unpretentious, sparkling, good-natured, and perfectly crafted little satellite plays, I would invoke a name which has not, so far, been joined to Kotzebue: that of Cervantes, whose *Entremeses* (Interludes) are distinctly more valuable than any of his grand plays except *La Numancia*. The two men share a common spirit of modest, sunny merriment, a delight with little pleasures, a keen sense for homely things, and a fondness for pranks and feather-light satire. It may be significant that the twelve playlets in our imaginary anthology were all printed in several of Kotzebue's annual *Almanacs*— volumes containing a cluster of dramatic pieces dashed off for home consumption. What this suggests to me is that Kotzebue belongs essentially to a class of artists whose minor works, irreverently concocted and scantly regarded by their creators, finally eclipse the elaborate monuments on which they staked their reputation. One such monument we do allow Kotzebue. Perhaps three. But for the rest, he was at his best when he carved small.

2

The Last Neoclassical Comedy

Aside from the autonomous aesthetic value—high or low—of *Die deutschen Kleinstädter*, Kotzebue's comedy occupies a noteworthy place in the history of dramatic literature; noteworthy, but as yet, I believe, unnoticed. Much has been written about the general historical importance of Kotzebuan dramaturgy. He is recognized as a fountainhead of ideas and techniques—of minor aesthetic value, to be sure (out of Kotzebue comes Scribe, for instance), but of major significance to the development of nineteenth-century drama. But *Die deutschen Kleinstädter* as such, taken by itself, is not—except for its decisive influence on Gogol—a fountainhead. It is a terminus. I see it as the last valuable neoclassical comedy in Europe. If "families" of literature exist at all, the one made up of memorable neoclasssical comedies may be said to begin with *La Mandragola* and to terminate with *Die deutschen Kleinstädter*. After the latter come Gogol, Nestroy, Labiche with a new, a "bourgeois" family; while in its own day a rival clan, that of the Romantic comedy of Tieck, Musset and so many others, scornfully disaffiliates itself from the tradition with which Kotzebue kept faith.

The briefest of summaries will set *Die deutschen Kleinstädter* in that tradition, the roots of which stretch back to Terence. The pretty and clever Lotte has fallen in love with Olmers, a promising young Berliner, while on a journey to the capital from her backwater of Krähwinkel (our Piffelheim). Her father, however—the town's Mayor—and her grandmother have promised her to a local versifying fool called Sperling. Tomorrow they are to be officially engaged, and the occasion will be a double one, for a female cattle-thief is to be clapped in the pillory after spending nine years in a cell. Olmers arrives from Berlin on the eve of the engagement. At first, however, he is mistaken by the family for the King travelling incognito (Lotte has kept Olmers' very existence a secret). When this is cleared up, he presents himself as a rival for Lotte's hand. The fact of the previous engagement does not trouble the Mayor, the grandmother, and two cousins; but what makes his candidacy impossible is that he bears no title of any sort. To be untitled in Piffelheim is to go naked. In a quandary, the two lovers play a trick on Sperling so that they can at least meet alone at night, namely in front of the house. There, however, they are surprised and exposed. At this point the turnkey comes running and clamoring that the delinquent has escaped. The Mayor trembles at the idea of severe sanctions from

Berlin. Olmers interposes: he is a friend of the Prime Minister, and promises to placate the authorities, provided Lotte becomes his wife. Everybody is satisfied, and as for Sperling, he no longer wants a girl who has lost her reputation by being found in the street at night talking to a man.

As is true of Molière's comedies, this recitation of the bare facts gives little promise of aesthetic satisfaction; but it serves to show to which literary family the play belongs. What then are the defining features of this group of comedies? We begin with an absence: the absence of sentimentality. In Germany the tide of easy tears, which had left minor comic writers like the two Gottsched and Johann E. Schlegel unaffected, toppled its first great bastion in Lessing's *Minna von Barnhelm*. Before 1765, Lessing had written several pure neoclassical comedies—mediocre ones, unfortunately, like *The Misogynist*. *Minna von Barnhelm*, with human qualities that raised it immediately above all its German competitors, still owed a geat deal to the "cool" tradition, but its most impressive scenes were written in the new spirit; scenes of self-denial and declamatory virtue made for a delicious *attendrissement*. From that moment on, victory was assured for the *apparently* classical comedy into which, sooner or later in the action, the new sensibility penetrated. A random example among hundreds is Heinrich Beck's *Das Kamäleon*, printed in the same year as *Die deutschen Kleinstädter*. Here the vivacious and wealthy Irene, determined to marry a beau of her own choice and not her father's, makes herself amusingly unbearable to a row of would-be suitors, insulting one, playing the idiot with another, gushing aggressively over a third, and so on. The scenes devoted to her are firmly obedient to the classical tradition. But athwart these scenes are others, featuring the melancholy and penniless Josepha, who sacrifices herself so that her equally penniless (though noble) lover can marry a wealthy heiress—none other, of course, than Irene who luckily does not want him. Here is a sample.

> JOSEPHA . . . Bring happiness to a wife who is worthy of you. Greet me now and then, and say a friendly word to me! . . . I won't deny that on your wedding day my woman's heart will urge a few tears to my eyes; but I shall be praying for your happiness—and—(*her tears prevent her from continuing*) Alas! they are flowing already. . . .
> EDVARD (*with an expression of the highest admiration*). Unrivalled soul![1]

And so forth. This was the *Minna*, *Werther*, and *Menschenhass* voice. The public—aristocratic, middle-class, and popular, as Professor Stock has so clearly shown[2] —loved it; and, with reservations, so did the intellectual elite.

[1] H. Beck, *Das Kamäleon*, Frankfurt a/M 1803, I, 7.
[2] Stock 1971, chapter 7.

What Lessing lastingly corrupted, Kotzebue briefly restored, thus playing the same role in Germany as Sheridan in England. But of course other essential neoclassical characteristics appear in *Die deutschen Kleinstädter*. It is a perfectly traditional marriage comedy. The lovable young are opposed to the unlovable old, the latter, as always, pig-headedly trying to arrange marriages the young want no part of. Two *raisonneurs* (Lotte and Olmers) explicitly assert a firm norm of values and behavior. Deviants are ridiculed for their aberration from it. Tricks are played: the clever fool the fools. Openly or by implication, intelligence, wit, elegance, and sophistication appear as prized values. And the tone is sprightly throughout—a cool, Haydn-like voice, carefully limiting its range and intensity. For to the classicist, "enthusiasm" is still a defect in the voice, associated, perhaps, with ranting popular preachers.

It will be understood that any given neoclassical comedy will not necessarily display all the characteristics of the family. In *Die deutschen Kleinstädter*, for instance, the roguish servant we tend to expect in such a play is missing. What happens instead—typically—is that his or her chief function, which is to devise and carry out the liberating trick, is taken over by the protagonists themselves.

Neoclassical comedy does not always pit the young against the old. Sometimes the intrigue depends on rival youths and/or rival maidens without an active, or decisive, presence of their elders. A special case, furthermore, is that of Marivaux, in whose most characteristic comedies the opponent to happy love has been internalized: it is a psychological obstacle which (like a father or superego) has to be tricked out of harm's way.[3] Then again, in a number of comedies, the deviation motif is so dominant that it reduces the marriage plot to a vestige. It may also happen (as, for instance, in Goldoni's *I malcontenti*) that the deviants are the young people and the raisonneur the old man. Most important, a whole subclass of neoclassical comedy dispenses with the moral-satirical-instructive motif of deviation altogether and confines itself to the merry trick: an intrigue concocted by the clever people to bring about the desired marriage or seduction. Our prototype here is Machiavelli's thoroughly Boccaccian farce, which also reminds us that the older man—or sometimes simply the unattractive male character—can be not only a father, uncle, guardian and the like, but also a husband. Typically for this subclass, the dolt's stupidity is treated as an immedicable defect—like a fact of Nature—and not as a moral deviation to be set straight inside or outside the fiction.

Despite all these possible variations, neoclassical comedies retain a strong family flavor. They share in a common commitment to the marriage or seduction plot, rivalries and generation-conflicts, tricks, disguises and mistaken identities; they value reason and common-sense; they applaud intelligence and wit; they stand for decorum and for elegance; they are loyal to the middle and upper

---

[3] See Mandel, *Seven Comedies by Marivaux*, Ithaca 1964 (reprint 1984), pp. 8-9.

classes of society; and they immerse themselves in a cool unsentimental atmosphere and a moderate emotional weather.

Let us look a little longer at *Die deutschen Kleinstädter*. In the wake of Molière, and under the guidance of J. C. Gottsched, the critic and playwright who tried all his life to reform German comedy along "regular" French lines, German writers had produced a series of moralizing comedies, each of which concentrated on some quirk or vice—usually in the older character, as I have indicated, but sometimes in one of the younger ones, as in fact Alarcón had already done in his *La verdad sospechosa* (The Liar, 1630). There were plays about the busy idler, the sensitive man, the witling, the inquisitive fellow, the ingrate, the slanderer, the trouble-maker, and so on. Anything Molière had left untouched in his too brief career was fair game.[4] That all these comedies were drearily schematic and lifeless is another story, which is not our concern here. One of the achievements of the Dane Ludwig von Holberg was to insert the traditional plot (in one form or another) into a thick social milieu—something Molière and his successors had not attempted. In *Den Elleste Junii*, for instance (The Eleventh of June, 1723), we are led into the Copenhagen Exchange, with "as many people on stage as there is room for," says the stage direction. Here, once a year, the thick-headed, griping merchants of Jutland arrive to collect moneys due to them by city folk. Holberg's plot consists in a series of extravagant tricks, requiring a dozen accomplices, and orchestrated by the traditional roguish servant, through which the young hero strips his cloddish creditor of all his possessions. The comedy clearly belongs to the "pure intrigue" subspecies of neoclassical comedy, where victory goes to intelligence and alertness; but we can see that a play of this kind opens the door to *Die deutschen Kleinstädter*, where again—with fewer actors on stage, to be sure—we deal with a group-antagonist rather than Molière's individual. The next step is to turn this group into a mass-deviant from a norm—a norm asserted and preserved either by one or two raisonneurs, or by another segment of society. This is a highly significant development—perhaps the only truly major development which neoclassical comedy underwent. With Molière, it is taken for granted that the group in the implied background—society, in a word—is "normal" and worthy of audience-approbation.[5] Next comes the notion of opening the theatrical scene itself to an entire social group—but as yet in a mere trick-play. This done, the group can become a mass aberrant from the norm, and the comedy shifts from a satire against individual vices and follies like avarice, hypocrisy, don-juanism, or hypochondria to a comical attack on an overall social condition.

[4] See in this connection Holl 1923, p. 127.

[5] In *The Misanthrope* Molière came close to repudiating society; but as if a little voice had whispered to him that Romanticism was not due for another century and more, and that the time for Childe Harold alienations was not yet, he faltered, and made his masterpiece so ambiguous that to this day critics wrangle over the question whether Alceste or society is the "sinner" of the piece.

Holberg's *Barselstuen* (The Lying-In Room, 1723 and 1731), though in itself a mediocre comedy, takes the decisive step I have mentioned. It satirizes a middle-class mania, that of raising a dreadful fuss of visiting, bringing gifts, bestowing compliments, and in general making life impossible for husband and wife alike for six weeks after a child is born. Here are no tricks, no victory over fools, no disguises. Holberg preserves a rudimentary jealousy motif (old husband-young wife), but almost the whole body of the play consists in a ship-of-fools parade in which the satirized social situation is displayed before our eyes.

A far better play in which a group once again deviates from a norm (upheld, in this instance, by a single character) is Goldoni's wonderfully funny *Le smanie della villegiatura* (roughly: Holiday Uproar, 1761). Upon a tenuous rival-lovers plot, Goldoni has draped the tapestry of a middle class turning its life topsy-turvy to "keep up with the Jones'" at summer homes in the country. Petty rivalries, imprudent debts, competition over dresses and festivities and guests, the shame of staying behind in town, etc. make up the elements of an annual mass insanity. Like Holberg before and Kotzebue after him, at the end of the play Goldoni leaves his fools to their folly. To do otherwise would be to begin the lurch into sentimentality: people do not in fact reform that easily.

In *Die deutschen Kleinstädter* we have, to begin with, the successful creation of a group. Without enrolling a crowd of actors, Kotzebue gives us a vivid sense of all-Piffelheim. The on-stage characters continually refer to and draw in the town's citizenry, and a delegation, knocking at the door, provides a bridge between those we see and those who populate the background. But the play rises above those of Holberg and Goldoni by virtue of the much greater importance of the aberrations which are held up to ridicule. *Title-mania* and *civic corruption* strike most of us as larger issues than fussing over new mothers or making a good show at a holiday resort. Other things being more or less equal, as here in fact they are, the more substantial the issue, the better the work of art; and this is true whether the problem is treated somberly, savagely, or smilingly.

Civic corruption remains at the periphery of the play, though highly visible. Gogol will be drawing this issue to the center of his masterpiece. At the center of *Die deutschen Kleinstädter* is the lust for titles which afflicts all the well-to-do citizens of Piffelheim except its raisonneur, Lotte. Kotzebue had had occasions enough to observe this mania in various places, notably at Reval, and we can detect more than a trace of it in himself—and in ourselves too, if we are at leisure to look. It so happened that in the German-speaking world the avidity for audible earthly honors had taken on an extravagance peculiar to these lands, and widely noted by travellers. Madame de Staël is often quoted:

The ancient forms of politeness, still in full force almost all over Germany, are contrary to the ease and familiarity of conversation; the most inconsiderable titles, which are yet the longest to be pronounced, are there bestowed and repeated twenty times at the same meal; etc.[6]

[6] Staël 1814, Part I, chapter 11.

It follows that the issue was a natural one for a German Molière, and natural it seems that Kotzebue's mind leaped in that direction while translating L. B. Picard's *La petite ville* (The Small Town, 1801), which does not deal with titles at all and yet inspired Kotzebue to write his own play.[7] John Murray's standard *Handbook for Northern Germany* drew attention to this mild national lunacy throughout the nineteenth century, in edition after edition, and even referred its readers to Kotzebue's comedy. But the Germans, obviously, merely intensified an all too normal and universal ambition, as Lotte herself remarks in the play. "The love of titles," Trollope wrote in *The Warden* (chapter 19), "is common to all men, and a vicar or fellow is as pleased at becoming Mr. Archdeacon or Mr. Provost, as a lieutenant, at getting his captaincy, or a city tallow-chandler in becoming Sir John on the occasion of a Queen's visit to a new bridge." Trollope's words suggest what lies, ultimately, behind Piffelheim title-mongering: simply the devouring human love of power. *Die deutschen Kleinstädter* expresses this lightly but unmistakably. And we have no trouble at all translating the farcical titles it revels in into titular assertions of power all our own.

I have called *Die deutschen Kleinstädter* the last valuable neoclassical comedy in Europe. The stress is on "valuable," for after all families of literature do not vanish at the stroke of a bell, they dwindle away. As is to be expected, aside from *Die deutschen Kleinstädter* a diminishing swarm of unsentimental-ized comedies can be detected on either side of the year 1800. In France, for instance, Picard kept Molière's banner doggedly aloft. In *Le Collatéral*, for instance—reputedly his best work, dated 1800—a false heiress is produced long enough to pry loose an engagement between the heroine and the legatee who has been forced on her: in a word, a grand trick is played by the clever on a power-ful fool. In the German world the tradition was kept feebly alive in such plays as F. W. Ziegler's *Liebhaber und Nebenbuhler in einer Person* (Lover and Rival in the Same Person, 1791), C. F. Bretzner's *Komplimente und Wind*, 1792,[8] J. F. Junger's *Die Geschwister vom Lande* (The Sisters from the Countryside, 1794), A. J. von Guttenberg's *Das Glass Wasser*, 1802, and August von Steigentesch's

---

[7] The hero of *La petite ville* has fled wicked Paris and his supposedly faithless mistress, and hopes to find more virtue in a small town. There, however, he meets with a series of unlovely "types" (the amorous spinster, the perpetual litigant, the gossip, etc.) and thus discovers that there is no difference between the provinces and Paris. Kotzebue translated the play shortly after it appeared, and it en-joyed a very modest run in Berlin in 1802 before his own comedy eclipsed it. A few details owed to Picard are mentioned in my notes to the play. But what clearly happened, as Kotzebue was translat-ing, is that Picard's play woke him to the possibility of doing *something* of his own centered on a provincial town and a capital. My guess is that his affection for Berlin gave him the "spin" that led him away from Picard's equation of small town and capital. The French playwright, director and ac-tor is forgotten today, but he was prominent enough while he lived. No less a man than Schiller translated two of his comedies.

[8] Bretzner wrote the libretto for Mozart's *Abduction from the Seraglio*. Several of Mozart's operas are of course neoclassical comedies set to heavenly music.

Der Briefwechsel (The Exchange of Letters, 1808). But such plays no longer set the rules of the game. Anyone who has the stamina to examine scores upon scores of forgotten scripts which had their day on stage and in print—or, for that matter, an acknowledged classic like Moratin's *El si de las niñas* (When a Girl Says Yes, 1805)—will be struck by the predominance of sentimental adulteration. A sturdy tradition which had, perhaps, survived long enough, was visibly dying, and a viable new family was not yet born.

As for Kotzebue, willing and able to turn out tearful comedies and anything else that might do on stage, it never occurred to him (as far as we know) either that *Die deutschen Kleinstädter* might be valued above all his other works, or that it concluded a chapter in the history of comedy. In his laconic preface to the printed play, he made the only point which mattered to him: his enemy A. W. Schlegel lacked the talent to write a comedy as good as his.

To complete the picture, something should be said about the bourgeois comedy which became the next successful family of comic drama. In this next phase, the marriage plot recedes. It never disappears, of course, but even where it remains in place, it is often caricatured or parodied, with almost grotesque figures replacing the attractive young couples of classical comedy. By the same token, the generation conflict is often replaced by the motif of suspected adultery—but not the adultery of the *Mandragola*, Cervantes' *Interludes*, or the *commedia*, where the young wife cuckolds her elderly Pantaloon. In the typical Feydeau comedy, for example, husband and wife are a normal married couple, and the husband is an average professional man of means. I do not need to dwell on the changed social realities which underlie such evolutions.

The new comedy tends to lose interest in the traditional deviant from a norm which is formulated by a raisonneur, leaving these edifying ways to the semi-comic, semi-serious *drame*. Tricks are still occasionally played; however, instead of pitting the clever trickster (master or servant) against the fool, the newer comedy tends to depict all its characters as fools; and as often as not these fools get themselves into the most awful and complicated scrapes unaided, by virtue of sheer imbecility. The classical presence *on stage* of a commanding intellect—the smart hero or heroine, the plain-spoken raisonneur, or the trickster—becomes a rarity.

New territories are opened: settings, trades, professions, nationalities, political affairs hardly touched by the very reserved classical drama. To be sure, both Holberg and Kotzebue are already exploring and innovating, but this only shows that in the arts, new families always inherit some of their materials from those which are beginning to decline. This is demonstrated, too, by the hugely increased number and importance of props in nineteenth-century comedy. British comedy was always generous with *things*—one recalls, for example, the famous screen in *The School for Scandal*; and *Die deutschen Kleinstädter* is rich enough in homely objects shown or mentioned to be of use to a social historian. But in the course of the century the stage fills out with as much furniture and objects as the spectators enjoyed in their own homes; and these often come alive, in the sense that they play a decisive role in the drama. Now it is a pair of spectacles, now a balustrade that needs to be installed, now a straw hat, now a pick-axe, now a dentist's chair. And local events are quickly seized upon: a new roller-coaster at the fair, a new card-game, a new piece of legislation. . . .

This rapid sketch suffices, I hope, to indicate the frontier—allowing for useful percolations, of course—between the decaying tradition and its aesthetically successful replacement. That *Die deutschen Kleinstädter* should here and there anticipate new tendencies comes as no surprise. And we can conclude by noting again the sharply drawn images of civic corruption, chicanery, and petty ambition in Kotzebue's play—a remarkable advance over his predecessors' range of allusion—which Gogol, inaugurating, as it were, the new era in a play emptied of raisonneurs, lacking attractive lovers, and inhabited only by fools and rogues, will presently absorb and exacerbate.

3

Kotzebue's Politics

Writing about *Die deutschen Kleinstädter* in his work on Iffland and Kotzebue, Karl-Heinz Klingenberg upbraided the latter for his failure to promote class-consciousness when, after all, he had the chance to do so in his comedy. "He does not bare the social and political roots of small-town doings, and prettifies where he ought to unmask and accuse."[1] This reproach was taken up and expanded by Hans Schumacher in his edition of the play. Kotzebue, we are told, "neither wished nor was able to hit the bourgeois' vulnerable spots." He could never "strike at the roots of the bourgeoisie." Consequently, his comedy remains trivial *Unterhaltung*—mere entertainment (always, as I have said already, a magic word in German criticism), and *Die deutschen Kleinstädter* comes off as the complacent snapshot "of a society which has lost its center and turns in a circle with empty formulas and indifferent amusing situations."[2]

Marxist critics of this sort would surely be surprised to hear that they are the direct descendants of intellectuals as peremptory as themselves—people like Tieck, Eichendorff, Madame de Staël, Hebbel and many others—who damned Kotzebue for his moral shortcomings with respect to sex and marriage. Here, to remind us of these strange bygone times, is Hebbel writing in his diary:

> Saw *Pagenstreiche* (The Page's Tricks) this evening at the Hofburgtheater. What a play! And what indecencies! A drunkard invites a person to bed with him in all seriousness, a person he believes to be a chambermaid, and even says, as he leaves, Follow me quickly! And our fine public has no objections to this, accepts all that dirt, and, I suppose, reassures itself on the ground that the person whose services have been solicited is a man, hence there can be no danger. O the hypocrisy of our times![3]

All we need do is change the terms of our indignation, and we become Marxist critics, that is to say political instead of sexual moralists. Imagine, we shall say, portraying a hungry woman who tried to steal a cow nine years ago and has been sitting in jail ever since waiting to be slapped into the pillory—imagine

[1] Klingenberg 1962, p. 140.
[2] Schumacher 1964, pp. 92 and 96.
[3] Quoted in Albertsen 1978, p. 223.

portraying this glaring example of the oppression of the proletariat without calling for blood in the streets! And so forth. So the world bumbles from one moral doctrine to another, each in turn making conditions and stipulations for the artist. I grant, to be sure, that to object to Grundyish and Marxist art-decrees is to adopt yet another moral doctrine—to sit upon a moral throne from which the others are anathematized. But a virtue that commends itself to almost every critic (I think) is critical clarity. In this particular instance, let the Marxists preface their aesthetic decision against our play with an explicit statement to the effect that a literary work which fails to be Jacobin (to use the term current in Kotzebue's life) when it could be so is *thereby* aesthetically damaged. Once this axiom is posited in black on white, honesty returns to the critical act.

The present work, as can be guessed, addresses itself to readers who no more demand left-wing political views before they delight in a literary text than they require belief in the Trinity or virgin heroines. If we were to belittle *Die deutschen Kleinstädter*, it would be either for some other wickedness (according to a moral creed we should have the lucidity and honesty to declare beforehand); for stupidity; or for purely artistic errors.

Other critics have accused Kotzebue of intellectual opportunism—of adopting any opinion in his plays that would tickle the fancy of his audience. This *ad hominem* charge began to be heard early in Kotzebue's career. In Schlegel's *Triumphal Arch*—already mentioned, and to be discussed again in the next section—the trigger-happy critic sneers at Kotzebue for being both a scandalous sans-culotte *and* an impudent aristocrat. The very monarchs who patronized Kotzebue were sometimes in doubt, for he seemed to reserve one quill for radical and another for reactionary utterances. With several other charges against his morals hung round his neck already, this one was easily believed of him; the man was known to be without scruples.

From the point of view which governs this essay, it is of course immaterial to the quality of a work of art whether its political or any other opinions are consistent with those expressed by the author in other works. Only *within* a text does inconsistency usually cause aesthetic damage. I am tempted, therefore, to drop that particular issue on the basis of gross irrelevance to my first concern, which is to create what I have called an aesthetic space for a single comedy. However, a second object of this volume is to recall to memory the once-famous man *as* a man; and Kotzebue was so consummately a political creature that his political views do, after all, deserve a few separate remarks.

As it happens, these views were as consistent, coherent, and indeed unchanging as they can ever be in mortal man. They were perhaps not very profound, and they were certainly not original (nor meant to be), but they had the merits of comprehensiveness, intelligence, and durability. Kotzebue was born into and never ceased to speak for the interests of the prosperous and still rising middle class: a class favored by, and in turn supporting, an enlightened monarch, that is to say a ruler surrounded by a responsible aristocracy, tolerant with respect to religion, averse to censorship, interested in economic productivity, and paternally protective of the lower classes. Let me repeat that I am addressing readers in whose minds, like mine, this set of social positions is compatible with works of art of the highest quality. Once this position is secured, we can move outside the aesthetic arena and attempt to explain why Kotzebue's contemporaries thought him politically shifty. The truth is that for him both the Right and the Left were enemies to the social, political, and economic order he favored. On the Right were despots, religious bigots, and unproductive aristocrats resting on their ancestors' laurels and bearing titles emptied of merit; on the Left were the Jacobins, the ignorant, bloodthirsty rabble and their leaders. Kotzebue was a singularly humane person, horrified by cruelty and, for a pugnacious writer, surprisingly fair-minded and good-humored. By temperament, therefore, he came easily to his dislike of the know-nothing aristocracy, arrogant to the bourgeois—that was bad enough—but also responsible for the suffering of the poor. On the other hand, an abrupt take-over of the world by the masses seemed monstrous. Kotzebue was at best skeptical about humanity in the aggregate. (His skepticism, we might note in parentheses, conveniently justified him in his own eyes for writing pot-boilers). Inevitably, the notion of peasants running City Hall or the Opera House looked to him like a criminal absurdity. He had seen Paris at the height of the Revolution, and again under the First Consul, and he had shuddered at the cruelties he witnessed and heard of. Unlike, say, John Dryden, who prudently (yet who can blame him?) changed his colors with those of his rulers, Kotzebue thus remained firmly a "centrist," and felt—I believe in all sincerity—that the Prussian model evolved after Frederick the Great—specifically, the moderate kingdom of Frederick William III, who had succeeded to the throne in 1797—was what mankind needed.[4] From that steadfast position, he aimed his arrows equitably at the two extremes, and thus gave many observers the impression that he believed in nothing, and was willing to make-believe he believed in anything.

Because—for reasons we will come to by and by—Kotzebue increased the volume of his anti-democratic writings in the last years of his life, his reputation as an opportunist shifted to the right after he was assassinated, and he came to be looked upon as an outright reactionary. For those who accept this verdict, it must surely come as a surprise that from the beginning to the end of his career as playwright he belabored with his Harlequin stick despots, useless lords, and the oppressive rich. His good noblemen are those who admire and sometimes adopt the bourgeois way of life. In *Die deutschen Kleinstädter* the citizens are satirized because, instead of governing wisely, they parrot the most sterile aspect of the feudal order, the glorification of titles. Lotte pointedly observes that in the nation's capital, titles are used only for official business; one does not

---

[4] See p. 95.

parade them anymore. But the most startling manifestation of Kotzebue's attitude appears in his supposedly grovelling tract *On the Aristocracy*, published in 1792, when he badly needed Catherine II's help. Somehow he slipped in this mischievous paragraph about the aristocracy he was praising:

> In our enlightened times Nobility is not lost because of the following things: when one contracts debts and does not pay them; when one seduces innocent girls and deserts them; when one begets illegitimate children and then takes no further thought of them; when one kills a friend in a duel; when one is idle and stupid.[5]

But lest this suggest that Kotzebue was an undercover Jacobin, it should be noted that he had recently published two rough (and extremely silly) comedies directed against egalitarians and revolutionaries: the notorious *Doctor Bahrdt*, and his *Female Jacobin-Club*. Perhaps a busy public—and a tsar or two, along with the Habsburg emperor—should not be blamed for misunderstanding these veerings. In a tragic era they seemed to denote at the very least a reprehensible levity. Paul I had Kotzebue dragged off to Siberia—then made amends; Francis II had Kotzebue dogged by a spy in Vienna—then made amends. It was hard to grasp that the mercurial fellow was, with perfect consistency, fighting the good centrist fight on two fronts.

If Kotzebue is to be faulted for anything at all in his political thinking, it must be for failing to grapple with the problem of what to do about tyrants other than hope they would all come to resemble the Prussian king, and, while waiting, satirize them without risking the gallows. This is not profound thinking, but we are dealing, after all, with a comic playwright, not with a philosopher; and for a comic playwright he had a solid hold on a comprehensive ideal for a social and political order. At any rate, few writers ever took greater pleasure in needling despots while looking innocent. The sultans of his Oriental fables (a good eighteenth-century tradition) are all transparent images of familiar tyrants—cruel, self-admiring, bored, and of course adamant against hearing uncomfortable truths. They reappear throughout his career: *Sultan Wampum* in 1795, *Sultan Bimbambum* in 1804, *The Princess of Cacambo* in 1815—with dialogue more or less after the following pattern:

HUSSEIN. You'll talk differently in a few days.
ALMA. And *think* differently too?
HUSSEIN. That you will do as you like.
ALMA. I shall never speak otherwise than I think.
HUSSEIN. You'll do best not to think at all, for here at court talk is

[5] Kotzebue 1978, p. 203.

abundant and thinking non-existent. (*Sultan Wampum*, II, 9)

But our Figaro-Kotzebue nagged at injustice and oppression in many a play which stayed closer to home. Here is a representative bit of dialogue from *Der Rothmantel* (The Red Coat, 1817), based on a tale by Musäus. The hero, a native of Bremen, is in Antwerp talking to a Flemish broker:

FRANZ. And do you have . . . laws and officials here?
BRAAM. And how! In our law-courts no rich man has ever pleaded his case in vain.
FRANZ. But the poor?
BRAAM. Ah yes, the poor, like everywhere else—justice is not for them.

In other plays, the oppressive tyrant is simply the local squire or his wife. Take, for example, the wealthy, wicked old spinster Rosamund in *Der Russe in Deutschland* (The Russian in Germany, 1805) reacting to a virtuous maidservant:

ROSAMUND. Godless creature! So cheeky and yet so young. Such are the consequences of the accursed Enlightenment. Once upon a time, when the master commanded, the common people obeyed. Now the lackey asks Why? Now the peasant wants to think; and though you put him in the yoke like every other animal, he has the gall to call himself a human being just like us. (I, 3)[6]

Later in the same play Rosamund meditates again on the peasant:

ROSAMUND. He belongs to an inferior race; an animal endowed with a rare spark of reason; in short, an animal fit only for our yoke. If we give him some potatoes and a Sunday sermon, our duty towards him is done. (III, 9)

About the time this little play was written, new constitutions were being considered for the Baltic lands governed by Russia. Kotzebue's comments on the project for Estonia, inserted at the start of the reminiscences of his journey to Italy, are pertinent. After raising a cloud of incense over the figure of Alexander I, he proceeds with a cautious objection to the proposed constitution. It appears that the peasants will preserve their right to seek redress from oppression through three judicial levels; but at each level the court will be staffed by noblemen, and at the highest instance the verdict will brook no appeal. "Whatever the

---

[6] This play, the Oriental tales, and many others are in Kotzebue's delightful light verse.

uprightness and integrity of these men may be, it is not right and expedient that
an entire [social] class should be virtually cut off from the monarch; that every
path to the throne should be closed to it; and that, in consequence, this class
should be wholly delivered into the hands of its masters." Admittedly (Kotzebue
continues) each lord has instituted a peasants' court in which judges selected by
themselves hand down decisions; but the chief magistrate of these courts is
appointed by the lord himself. The result is that such courts dare not decide
against his wishes. "It is . . . as though a nobleman were to fill a tribunal with his
courtiers, and appoint one of his chamberlains as president of the court."[7]

A passage of this sort—which expresses the authentic Kotzebue beyond any
shadow of doubt—enables us to understand why this supposed reactionary never
wrote a "put-down" of the lower classes comparable, say, to Holberg's virulent
Jeppe of the Hill. Even when he attacked the extreme Left, his targets were
always their leaders and the intelligentsia. A letter dated June 1, 1810, addressed
from his Estonian lands to a friend whose identity is lost, and never meant for
publication, sums up, in a microcosm, the humane paternalism Kotzebue wished
on the world:

> I study and I write works of history, I tutor my children, I write farces for
> the stage, I cultivate my land with great zeal, and do as much for my
> peasants as is in my power. And thank God everything thrives. My chil-
> dren are making substantial progress. My peasants are better off every
> year. Through my example, donations of seed, and considerable prizes, I
> have succeeded in introducing large-scale potato-farming among them.
> They hate all novelties, and for a long time wanted no part of it. But
> already last fall, here at Schwarzen, where the yearly crop of potatoes never
> exceeded ten tons, 621 tons were harvested, and this year we may well dou-
> ble this figure. You would have to be familiar with the hunger which
> returns here year after year in order fully to appreciate this good deed of
> mine. In fact, it is generally acknowledged in my vicinity. This Spring a
> crowd of peasants from other parts requested seed from me, and several
> landowners are copying me. . . . At sowing-time I rode out in person to
> each, and myself planted the first row. They have a superstitious belief in
> my good luck. . . . Forgive me, dear friend. The thought that this unhappy
> people will be blessing me even after I die is so sweet, that I am prouder, I
> confess, of my potatoes than of everything I have written, my history of
> Prussia hardly excepted.[8]

[7] *Erinnerungen von einer Reise aus Liefland nach Rom und Neapel* (1805), in Kotzebue 1842, vol.
41, pp. 22-23. According to Rabany, these comments were suppressed by the censor in all but a few
copies of the original edition. I do not know whether they appear in the English translation, *Travels
Through Italy, in the Years 1804 and 1805*, published in London in 1806.
[8] In W. von Kotzebue 1881, pp. 159-160.

That this account, so reminiscent of Voltaire at Ferney, on the one hand, and of Tolstoy on the other, is not empty chat is attested by the fact that Kotzebue had founded an agricultural society in his region and become its secretary—an achievement to be set next to his rather more famous creation of a theater many years before at Reval. Today, condescensions like his infuriate friends of the working classes worse, on the whole, than mulish, shameless privilege; but in my own opinion, it yet remains to be proved that this approach to social and political problems was either less intelligent, or less conducive, to widespread human happiness, than revolutionary destruction and redistribution. However, such questions leave both our aesthetic and our biographical interests too far behind. To Kotzebue the man we therefore return.

4

A Life and a Death

One result of the antipathy "right-thinking" Germans have felt toward Kotzebue—Kotzebue the reactionary, the immoralist, the commercial hack, the quarreler, the pet aversion of the best minds of his day—is that no German has had the inclination to write a full life since 1830, when Heinrich Döring brought out a fair-minded account. A Frenchman—Charles Rabany—published a Life and Times of Kotzebue in 1893; again a sensible account, a useful supplement to Döring, but bringing to light no significant new materials. Rabany inspires awe, however, for having read ALL Kotzebue's plays, and, it would seem, nearly everything else the inexhaustible scribbler ever wrote. In recent years Professor Jürg Mathes has edited two large caches of Kotzebue letters, most of them hitherto unknown, to which he has attached an illuminating series of biographical notes—a wealth of information for which Kotzebue students must be deeply grateful. But it is clear that a new comprehensive Life is in order. What follows here is a mere sketch: some fresh thoughts, some new materials; more, in any event, than has ever been forthcoming in the English language. But it remains for a professional biographer to comb state and local archives in the many places where Kotzebue resided, or made his presence felt; to study the newspapers, periodicals and pamphlets of the time; and to search far more deeply than has been done so far through the correspondence, journals and memoirs of Kotzebue's contemporaries. Even if the literary rehabilitation of Kotzebue as the last worthwhile comic writer of neoclassical comedies is disavowed, other excellent reasons for writing a full Life remain: Kotzebue as a phenomenon of literary and social history, Kotzebue as a tragic mover in German history, and the dramatic interest of the story in itself.

The first chapter of the Life can be thought of as the period from Kotzebue's birth to the Bahrdt affair—an absurd literary scandal which broke over his giddy head in 1791.

August Friedrich Ferdinand Kotzebue (the *von* came later) was born in Weimar in 1761, the son of a well-placed official (*Legationsrat*) at the court of the Duchess Anna Amalia of Saxe-Weimar. Levin Karl Christian Kotzebue died two years after August's birth. The lad grew up under the loving care of his mother, who was to outlive him for eleven years, and altogether in a warm domestic cocoon from which he must have acquired his life-long and most attractive devotion to household affections. He found a sort of father-substitute in his uncle, the well-known fable-writer J. K. A. Musäus (1735-1787) who encouraged the boy in his first schoolroom literary efforts—for, indeed, the staggering flood of Kotzebuan ink began to flow almost as soon as the boy learned how to write. Early on, Musäus, who was Governor of the Pages, introduced him to the Weimar playhouse, where a strolling company was performing Klopstock's *Death of Adam*. "I came home stunned with delight. I was asked, how I liked the play? Ah, my God! LIKED!—What a feeble word to describe my feelings!"[1] Presently little Kotzebue was staging plays at home with his friends. When Anna Amalia installed a permanent professional company at Weimar, he became a passionate spectator. "Every corner of the house was as well known to me as the inside of my coat-pocket, even the passages under the stage were as familiar to me as to the man who lighted the lamps." He could repeat Lessing's *Emilia Galotti* by heart, and loved, next to it, *The Grateful Son* by J. J. Engel, to whom he was to pay a grateful compliment in *Die deutschen Kleinstädter*.

Late in 1775 Goethe settled in Weimar. The famous author of *Werther* became a friend of the family. Almost needless to say, young Kotzebue was overpowered by Goethe's novel. "I would readily have run my hands into the fire to retrieve Goethe's lost shoe-buckle." One memorable day, in a home-production, the boy played the Postillion vis-á-vis Goethe himself in the poet's recently written *Die Geschwister* (Brother and Sister). Another guest in the house was Klinger, the very man who coined the term *Sturm und Drang* in 1776. In short, Kotzebue grew up in the very best of circumstances, pampered, encouraged, surrounded by cultivated persons, and very much a lad of letters.

At the age of sixteen he left the maternal house for the University of Jena, where he immediately joined an amateur theatrical group. It is noteworthy that he played a role—a woman's role, on account of his youth—in one of the most successful and characteristic sentimentalizing comedies of the period: C. W. F. Grossmann's brand-new *Nicht mehr als sechs Schüsseln* (No More Than Six Dishes). Indeed, Kotzebue soon became familiar with much of the international repertory of the neoclassical comedy without, apparently, discriminating between its pure and its sentimentalized manifestations.

A year later we find him temporarily in the Rhineland town of Duisburg, studying law, organizing amateur theatricals, and—again on the alert for the latest—playing in a German translation of Sheridan's *The Rivals*. In 1779 he is once more at the University of Jena, near his mother's home in Weimar, and obtains his law degree there. But Weimar is full of lawyers already, and Kotzebue is *very* young. Shades of Virgil—we hear of only one client, a farmer not very happy to have a novice as his advocate, even though the beginner wins his case, whatever it was. What is clearly more important for Kotzebue is that

[1] Kotzebue 1800, p. 24.

he now publishes—encouraged as before by Musäus—a bit of fiction, a bit of poetry, a bit of drama. The year is 1781.

Why, it has been asked, did Kotzebue suddenly leave Weimar at this point? Biographers have offered an undignified reason, Kotzebue himself advanced a dignified one. As often happens, two truths may be better than one. The scale may have tipped in favor of departure when a grievance was added to a disgrace. The disgrace, it has been surmised, was occasioned by some lampoon in verse or dialogue—now lost—which the already then too merry Kotzebue directed against some of the Weimar ladies.[2] The grievance was recorded by Kotzebue in 1817—long after the event, to be sure, and yet with details, and frank admissions, which inspire confidence. It appears that Kotzebue had applied to the Herr Minister von Goethe for the post of War Secretary to Weimar's toy-shop army. Goethe, says Kotzebue, gave the post to one of his own assistants, but did so most uncivilly:

> Four times I sought an appointment in order to submit my request, but in vain, he did not receive me. As there was no time to lose, my loving mother decided to call on him herself. He was living in his garden-home, at some distance from the town. It was a very hot day. My mother went and I stayed home, anxiously awaiting her return. She came back sooner than expected; she sank into the sofa faint with fatigue and heat, and bathed in tears, for—Goethe, though at home, had had a servant dismiss her. Never will the picture fade from my soul of my exhausted, deeply wounded mother wiping the perspiration and tears from her face.

This account, I repeat, is credible—although, as there would be other occasions when the lady was to busy herself too zealously on her son's behalf, a guess can be ventured that Goethe had some ground for irritation even then. But why did not Kotzebue tell this story in 1796, when he wrote his first autobiographical piece? Why did he wait until 1817? The answer may simply be that in 1796 it was still in his interest to conciliate the powerful genius of Weimar. But in 1817, after years of disaffection, he could feel free to write "It was Goethe who threw me out into the world."[3]

Whatever the reasons, in the fall of 1781, helped by a well-placed friend of his late father, Kotzebue took the road, well-worn by talented and ambitious Germans, to St. Petersburg. There he entered the service of a German official, Baron von Bauer, himself in the service of the German-born Catherine II. As luck would have it, Bauer was presently appointed director of the German theater in the Russian capital. By February 1782 Kotzebue was the real man in charge, and as such saw to the production of his tragedy *Demetrius Ivanovich*,

[2] See Kahn 1951, pp. 75-76 for a summary in English.
[3] Kotzebue 1922, pp. 178-179.

Tsar of the Russians. This story of the false tsar proved unwelcome to the authorities, and we see him briefly in the first of many scrapes with censorship—in Russia, in Vienna, and in a number of German statelets.

St. Petersburg was a cosmopolitan center, boasting of an Italian, a French, and even a Russian theater in addition to the German company. It is probable that Kotzebue all but completed his education there in the international repertory of tragic, pathetic, and comic drama. In any event, the journey to Russia was decisive for him. He never lost sight of Weimar, but he became a Russian citizen, a Russian magistrate, a Russian nobleman, a Russian landowner, and, in the end, a sort of martyr (or spy, as his enemies would have it) in the Russian service—all this, it appears, without learning more than a few words of the language.

Already in St. Petersburg he was involved in one of the many quarrels that marred his entire career. An enemy circulated rumors that he was his noble benefactor's illegitimate son, and being groomed as a spy for Prussia. Kotzebue fought back, tattled indignantly and self-righteously wherever he was admitted, reported to his mother—in short, gives us a first look at the authentic personality: afflicted, in the words of his own doting mother, with a "cursed thoughtlessness," and in his own, with "morbidly irritable nerves." At the end of his life, he would write in a few terse words a summary verdict on this and many a later fracas: "Ich konnte nicht schweigen"—I could not keep my mouth shut.[4]

Baron von Bauer died shortly after Kotzebue took up his duties under him. The young man would have liked to inherit the direction of the German Theater, but this Catherine would not grant.[5] Instead, he was appointed to an honorable junior post on the bench at Reval (today Talinn) in the Russian but heavily Germanized province of Estonia. He assumed the robe in 1783. At the age of twenty-three he married the nobly born Friederike von Essen, whose father was instrumental in obtaining a quick promotion for her husband. Not yet twenty-four years old, Kotzebue was named "President" (presiding judge) of the high court of appeal and made a Russian nobleman: from this time on he is called von Kotzebue. He continued in this function until 1795, when he obtained his dismissal from service. He observed at that time in Reval a great deal of scrambling after titles—professing, of course, to be untouched by it himself—and he obviously remembered this when he wrote *Die deutschen Kleinstädter.*[6]

In one of his autobiographical fragments, Kotzebue allows us to glimpse him not in his judicial dignity but as a high-spirited lad of twenty-four gadding about with college students and playing an innocent prank on an older official. In the same spirit, he goes to a nearby town with some "merry youngsters" to act out a play, then gets the idea of organizing an amateur theater at Reval, where

---

[4] Kotzebue 1821, p. 75. The essay is appropriately titled, "How is it I have so many enemies?"
[5] Giesemann 1971, p. 28.
[6] Kotzebue 1922, p. 181.

admission will be charged, and the proceeds (in old Spanish fashion) distributed to the poor. As it turned out, this theater subsisted for some twenty-five years, and Kotzebue remained proud of his accomplishment. On the other hand, he confesses that a good many citizens were shocked "to see a man on stage today and on the judicial bench tomorrow."[7]

The curtain rises ever so briefly on a more elevated scene: "I remember now, that in 1793 the Empress Catherine abolished Estonia's old constitution, and introduced a new one with great pomp. I found myself among the new judges who, two by two, collectively wended their way to the church, led by the Governor, to take the oath."[8] The daily realities must have been more relaxed. Word reached Catherine about young Kotzebue's inattention to duty, but apparently she expressed her displeasure only in letters he never saw—as in this one, addressed to Melchior Grimm on March 3, 1791: "Kotzebue may be an admirable person and writer; but—to speak the truth—he gives no thought to his duties: he takes his salary but allows others to do his work."[9]

In his *Liebhabertheater* Kotzebue mounted plays of his own, works by Engel, Iffland, the Grossmann comedy mentioned before, and even a play by the Russian Empress. At the same time he was publishing a series of stories and novels (the only one to which I have seen some praise given is *Die Leiden der Ortenbergischen Familie*—The Sufferings of the Ortenberg Family, 1785, 1788), and editing a monthly called *Für Geist und Herz* (For Spirit and Heart, 1786)—his first sally into journalism. Now and throughout his life, this *touche-à-tout*, this touch-all, as a French writer has called him, seems to have had time for everything, including even leisure.

Presently too he was a father, and a loving one. A quizzical look at relevant dates shows that his good Friederike was pregnant when he married her. But here it may be said that as far as women were concerned—and little else— Kotzebue showed excellent emotional and practical sense all his life. Each of his three wives belonged to the Baltic nobility. Apparently he truly loved them and truly mourned the two who died before him. Granted, his remarriages took place with a rapidity which disconcerts a little. But, rather than a "most wicked speed," I see in this another manifestation of his quicksilver ways: nothing permanent, everything quick, a hop and a skip from one thing to another, with consequences, implications, and repercussions to think of tomorrow. Yet it seems clear that his wives and children (thirteen of whom can be counted at the time of his death) loved him as much as he cared for them. In short, not a single sour look emerges from his households.

Cozily domestic, he was nevertheless enough of an eighteenth-century blade to fill his comedies with merry thrusts at the married state. I assume that he

[7] Kotzebue 1821, pp. 96-101.
[8] Kotzebue 1842-1843, vol. 41, p. 78; in the 1805 account of his journey to Italy.
[9] Mathes 1969, p. 267.

explained them away to his fond wives by the fireside or in bed. He wrote effusively of Lucien Bonaparte, both in Paris and in Italy, because the Consul's brother was a devoted family man. At the same time, he failed to see in women any possibility worth attending to—except satirically—beyond their condition as nubile maidens, warm wives, and devoted mothers. Women, he declared, were not made for thinking. He had undoubtedly read, and inwardly approved of, the passage in Rousseau's *Letter to d'Alembert* in which the writer rhapsodizes: "Is there a more touching, praiseworthy spectacle in the world than that of a mother surrounded by her children, managing the work of her servants, securing a happy life for her husband, and wisely governing the household?" One regrets to say that Kotzebue's thinking on this subject was running in the very same groove a good fifty years after Rousseau's effusion.

During a period of sickness in the winter of 1788 he composed his *Menschenhass und Reue*. It received its premiere at his own theater in Reval in November of that year, and was played there again twice in 1789. But the pivotal day came at the beginning of June 1789 when J. J. Engel, director of the National Theater, produced the melodrama in Berlin. A sort of electric shock occurred—one which spread quickly in all directions. Suddenly Kotzebue was famous. Soon he would be perhaps the most popular playwright in the annals of the European drama. Years of enthusiasm for the theater, intelligent absorption of the tradition, high ambition, easily aroused emotions without passionate commitments, and a wonderfully fluent pen, combined somehow to create just what the mass audience wanted—and by "mass audience" I mean kings, lords and ladies, wealthy merchants, humble spectators—everybody except disgruntled intellectuals and, as we have seen, austere moralists—the two often combined in the same person.

Why should the conclusion of *Menschenhass*, which I exhibited a few pages back, have shocked "decent folk"? It seems so humanely innocuous to the modern reader that, for a moment, he is apt to feel as distant from his ancestors as if they belonged to another species. But it should be recalled that audiences absolutely expected from their serious plays—and paintings—a representation of horrid punishment for the least sexual deviation of their heroines, even if that deviation were forced on the girl by an omnipotent tyrant. A single slip, and the lady was undone. She must commit suicide, be executed by her father or husband, beg in the streets, flee to some Australia, turn prostitute, or (if lucky) spend her remaining sixty-odd years in the piacular abasement of a conventual cell. "Real life" was a far gentler affair, but for their fictions audiences liked the old verities upheld. Without seeking after origins, we can bracket *Menschenhass* between Nicholas Rowe's *Fair Penitent* (1703), where the heroine who sinned one fatal night stabs herself to death:

> And dost thou bear me yet, thou patient earth?
> Dost thou not labor with my murd'rous weight?

> And you, ye glitt'ring, heav'nly host of stars,
> Hide your fair heads in clouds, or I shall blast you,
> For I am all contagion, death and ruin,
> And nature sickens at me— (V, 228ff.)

between this and, perhaps, Little Em'ly in *David Copperfield*, not to mention numberless edifying paintings and prints of fallen females sobbing with useless remorse at the feet of their offended masters. German audiences could bear in mind Lessing's *Emilia Galotti* (1772), where the heroine is stabbed by her father, Roman fashion, even before she is violated by the vile seducer. And Goethe's Gretchen, who was shortly to be introduced to the world, would be hanged by the secular arm before being theologically saved. Forgiveness in heaven was by that time allowed. But it seemed intolerable that a female sinner should be forgiven on earth, *and* reunited with her doting husband, *and* live happily (one could tell) ever after. Intolerable and wonderful. For of course *Menschenhass* did "seduce" the large public. Many years would pass before a less Moorish view of female sexuality could impose itself on fictions (and when it happened at last, a tidal wave overswept all), but already Kotzebue had touched the more equitable sensibilities to come.

Menschenhass was but the first of a series of plays bold in their moral outlook though cheap enough as literature. In the wake of his first success he composed another egregious piece of sentimental melodrama called *Das Kind der Liebe* (The Child of Love, 1790, promptly translated three times in England under different titles but known more respectably as *The Lovers Vows*).[10] Here Kotzebue portrayed a rich seducer who marries the social inferior he had wronged many years before and unwittingly reduced to beggary—scandalously marries her and scandalously legitimizes his bastard son. Presently Kotzebue was showing off his *Bruder Moritz, der Sonderling* (Brother Moritz the Eccentric, 1790) where few, perhaps, noticed statements against freedom of the press and remarks to the effect that a woman's only business in life is to get married, while everyone was startled by Jacobin-sounding theories against hereditary aristocracy, by the hero's toying with the idea of marrying not one of his own sisters but two of them, and by his final decision to wed a maidservant and embrace, on stage, her illegitimate child by another man.

In his *Die Negersklaven* (The Negro Slaves, 1796) Kotzebue broadened his sweep and, inspired by William Wilberforce and the anti-slavery movement in general, launched a torrentially sentimental, declamatory, and melodramatic attack on the atrocities perpetrated by plantation-owners in Jamaica. Here is a bit of discussion between the wicked slave-owner John and his virtuous brother William:

---

[10] And still a shock fourteen years later to Jane Austen, whose hero and heroine are horrified by the notion of performing it *en famille* at Mansfield Park.

WILLIAM. Tell me, brother, do you consider your slaves to be human beings?

JOHN. I treat them as human beings.

WILLIAM (*derisively*). Really?

JOHN. I give them food and drink.

WILLIAM. This you give your dogs as well.

JOHN. And in fact they are not much better than dogs. Believe me, brother, they're a race that's born to be slaves.

WILLIAM. Where is the sign that God stamped them as slaves?

JOHN. They descend from Cain; they're black, because their ancestor was the first man to commit fratricide.

WILLIAM. Wonderful!

JOHN. They are mischievous, malicious and stupid. They themselves recognize the superiority of our spirit and therefore the justice of our dominion over them.

WILLIAM. They are stupid, because slavery destroys the soul; they are malicious, but not malicious enough against you people. They lie, because no tyrant should be told the truth. They recognize the superiority of our spirit, because we keep them in eternal ignorance, and the justice of our dominion over them, because we misuse their weakness. O you have done everything to abase these unhappy people, and then you complain that they are stupid and malicious.

. . . .

JOHN. I'll knock down your whole pseudo-philosophy with a single stroke: without us they'd never have known the Christian religion. They exchange their freedom for the salvation of their souls.

WILLIAM. O divine Creator! Had you foreseen how your gentle teachings would be be used to justify such abominations!—When religion sanctifies crimes, away with it forever! Speak up, you servants of the Church! Retort at the top of your voices! Here passion would be wisdom, and silence a crime. (I, 6)

Crying out against slavery was not a monopoly of Jacobins, but if we note that the French revolutionary government had abolished slavery in all French colonies in 1794 and conferred on Negroes the rights of French citizens (Kotzebue could not foresee that Napoleon would restore servitude in 1802), we can conclude that such humanitarian pleas, made in 1796, suggested leanings unwelcome to the enemies of the Revolution. Indeed, in spite of Wilberforce ("Blessings on the kind foreigner!" exclaims one of the slaves), the English did not abolish the slave trade until 1807, and slavery itself until 1833.

In *La Peyrouse* (also in 1796) we return to domestic naughtiness. On an island in the Pacific the shipwrecked hero has taken a beautiful native girl—in fact, a precursor to Byron's Haidee—for his bedmate. His virtuous wife, however, has sailed round the globe to find him, and find him she does, to the gentleman's consternation and joy. What to do? The solution is to keep the love-triangle happily in place. "The paradise of innocence!" is the play's final exclamation.[11] Twenty years later Kotzebue reworked the play and decorously ended it with the suicide of the native girl and the preservation of the orthodox marriage. He never really gave up toying in his plays with "equivocal" bedroom situations, but after *La Peyrouse* he confined his fooling to fluffy comedies, where, he must have thought, it would give less offense.

It may not be amiss to recall that these and other spicy works were written during the unedifying rule of Frederick William II of Prussia (1786-1797) who, while thoroughly reactionary in politics and religion, divorced one wife and married another, installed a permanent head mistress on the side (with the queen's approval), took a series of additional mistresses (with the ranking mistress's approval and connivance), and married two of them (the second after the death of the first) in the Lutheran church, thus becoming twice a bigamist. Kotzebue was a Russian citizen, to be sure, but only technically; his true center was Prussia, of which Weimar itself was a satellite; and surely the plays of the 1790's can be read by the scarlet glow emanating from the court of Berlin and nearby Potsdam. Be that as it may, Kotzebue did advance some radical notions in the plays he wrote in this decade. Modern critics would probably have admired him for doing so if he had not irritated them by fighting the later radicals.

With *La Peyrouse*, we have now run a few years ahead of the story. Let us return to the time of *Menschenhass*. Kotzebue was shocking the moralists, filling theaters, and defending himself by citing cases of tender reconciliation or returns to virtue occasioned by his play.[12] Directors everywhere made flattering offers. The royal house in Berlin fawned over him—in short, he had consolation aplenty for hostile notices (especially from Weimar) and for digestive problems which led him three summers in a row to the waters of Bad Pyrmont, not far from Hanover.

---

[11] Goethe had preceded Kotzebue in his picture of a threesome in *Stella* (1776); and Mathes (1972, p. 565) gives several other examples of this erotic motif in Germany at the time. *La Peyrouse* had little success in Berlin, however, and was predictably banned in Vienna.

[12] Kotzebue 1840-1841, vol. 7, p. 53. Schneider 1927, pp. 180-181 reports an actor from Cadiz making the same sort of claim in 1811: "Many of the inhabitants of this noble city are witnesses to having seen the first representation of the play titled *Misanthropiá y arrepentimiento*, on the occasion of which many married couples who had separated over trifles were reunited and tied once more in the bonds of matrimony. And as a result of the production of *La Reconciliación de los dos hermanos*, sundry hostile families were appeased and forgot the domestic discords which had caused their enmity." This was the sort of ammunition Kotzebue liked to use, for he had no wish to pose as an outsider, a rebel—in a word, a Romantic.

In 1789, on his way from Pyrmont to Reval after a first summer at the spa, Kotzebue stopped in Berlin to enjoy the continuing success of *Menschenhass*. A letter to his mother, of which a large fragment survives, gives us an excellent notion of what the city meant to him already a dozen years before he had Olmers and Lotte praise it in *Die deutschen Kleinstädter*.

The fragment begins with the mention of an oratorio by Dittersdorf presented to the royal family in the opera house. Kotzebue is one of the guests. It goes on to recount a merry breakfast with Engel and Mrs. Unzelmann, Kotzebue's leading actress—making up, he writes, for a boring lunch to follow with Count Nesselrode. In the afternoon he calls on Prince Ferdinand, the reigning monarch's uncle, and other members of the royal family who are eager to make his personal acquaintance. He is extremely satisfied with the reception they accord him, especially, he adds, in view of the fact that the court still favors all things French and scorns German writers. A young Princess invites him to a ball in honor of the king's sister visiting from the Netherlands. He will be seated in the princess' own loge. "All this would not have happened to me in Weimar."

When an opera by Martin y Soler is performed, Kotzebue is seated in the loge of the chief ladies-in-waiting to the Queen. He dines with the theater crowd, Engel, and others. One morning he is obliged to sit for his portrait: the booksellers have been asking for it. Engel gives him a substantial bonus because of the success of *Menschenhass*, and emissaries from Vienna and Copenhagen pay him cash for the rights to his play. He attends a performance and is pleased to see a good crowd in the theater. After the play comes another jolly supper: "We made merry until late in the night." He is even granted three kisses by the adorable Unzelmann. But Kotzebue is no Frenchman. He has left Berlin with a heavy heart, but had he not some hosiery to bring home to his wife in remote Estonia—a gift from his honorable mother? Friederike "thankfully kisses her hand" for it.[13]

A letter Kotzebue received from Engel that winter, several months after his return to Estonia, adds color to our picture. The three plays the director mentions are all, of course, by Kotzebue.

> With what shall I begin? With what shall I end? I have seen *The Hermits*, I have read the beginning of *The Virgin of the Sun*, talked about you to the King. . . .
> From Potsdam the King ordered *The Indians in England* for the 17th of November, came [to Berlin] especially for the performance and then returned [to Potsdam]. That was surely the work of your friend, the Princess Friedericke, his beloved and lovable daughter, who is as fond of you as

[13] Mathes 1970, No. 5.

is the Princess Luise. After the play I accompanied the King, who showed himself extremely friendly and pleased, to his carriage. 'Kotzebue,' he said, 'has great genius; he ought to write more; tell him so!'—We hope, Your Majesty, to have a new play from him this very winter; so he promised me. 'What sort of play?'—Whether it will be a drama or a tragedy I cannot guess as yet; but it is one of the two. . . .

'You cannot believe,' said to me recently Princess Luise of her own accord, 'how much I talk about Kotzebue! The man must become one of us.' I hope to heaven he does! I said, and surely he won't deny us, thought I, when the time comes? Because it would be a terrible pity if the dear Princess Luise's well-intentioned efforts come to nought.[14]

An entry in the diary of Elisa von der Recke (1756-1833), among whose extensive literary contributions I note a volume of poems entitled *Elisa's Spiritual Songs*, allows us to catch sight of Kotzebue during his cure at Bad Pyrmont in 1790 "in a circle of ladies courting him." Bad Pyrmont, a rendez-vous for the rich, noble, and well-connected, had acquired a new theater in the 1780's. In 1790 Kotzebue's *Das Kind der Liebe* had left "not a single eye in the parterre dry." But then came a performance of *Bruder Moritz* by the famous Grossmann troupe of actors. The play had not yet appeared in print. If it had, the company might have been warned that Bad Pyrmont was not the place for its gallic notions. "A more immoral play," Elisa confided to her diary, "has never been performed in the German theater. I deeply rejoiced that all the ladies gathered at Pyrmont voiced their displeasure. After it was produced, the honorable Countess von Mecklenburg and our beloved Princess von Augustenburg treated Kotzebue with cold politeness. The Countess reproved him with noble dignity for this unworthy use of his fine talent."[15] For the biographer, the entry is precious because it shows Kotzebue as both the darling and the naughty imp of high society. For the rest, it is unlikely that the cold shoulder he was shown in certain quarters ("officially," at any rate) did anything to dampen his exuberance—the fatal hubris of the unbeatable winner; for while at Pyrmont that season, he perpetrated the bad joke that was to hound him for the rest of his life, and beyond.

One of the leading figures in the *beau monde* of Bad Pyrmont was the vainglorious Dr. Johann Georg Zimmermann, royal physician at Hanover, a favorite of Catherine II, and proud of having been called in to attend Frederick the Great in his last illness. His failure to do the king any good evidently made less noise than the honor of having been summoned to try. Zimmermann was some 33 years Kotzebue's senior, and had achieved European fame in the 1780's with a treatise on Solitude (*Von der Einsamkeit*, 1784-1785). He

---

[14] Kotzebue 1821, pp. 279-281. Princess Luise is the future queen-consort of Frederick William III, deservedly adored by her subjects. Princess Friedericke later became Duchess of York.
[15] Stock 1971, pp. 93-94, and Kuhnert 1984, pp. 191-192.

enthusiastically admired *Menschenhass*, and earned Kotzebue's gratitude when, in 1789, he procured from the tsarina a leave of absence with pay for the playwright so that the latter might take the summer cure for a couple of seasons. Zimmermann had been feuding for a long time with representatives of the Enlightenment, and many a literary blow had been given and taken on both sides. When the French Revolution broke out, he accused the liberals and radicals of having brought it about. One of these radicals, an unsavory but clever ex-professor and ex-clergyman by the name of Dr. Bahrdt published a libelous pamphlet against him. Unsolicited, Kotzebue decided to compose a merry counter-attack on behalf of his friend—personal gratitude mingling in his mind with his own anti-Jacobinism and, undoubtedly, an appreciation of the warm ties between Zimmermann and his own employer Catherine. Besides, Kotzebue was riding high; he was Fortune's pet, and ready for the prank of the decade. He quickly wrote and published his sophomoric, scatological farce entitled *Doctor Bahrdt mit der eisernen Stirn, oder Die deutsche Union gegen Zimmermann*, which translates as Doctor Bahrdt of the Iron Brow, or the German Conspiracy against Zimmermann (1790).[16] Instead of publishing it anonymously, he decided to give his enterprise a little more spice by ascribing authorship on the title-page—somewhat illogically—to yet another enemy of Zimmermann, a certain Knigge. In the farce itself, the pseudo-Knigge pilloried a small army of Zimmermann foes. Highly topical in addition to its other deficiencies, *Doctor Bahrdt* is of course indigestible today.

For a while the laugh was on Kotzebue's side, and he could secretly enjoy the fact that the public promptly bought up all the copies. He wrote to his publisher that he was ready for another prank. Presently, however, hubris met its usual fate; the joke turned sour. Zimmermann, the very opposite of a man of jokes, was appalled by this scurrilous defense of his dignified self. He even suffered the indignity of having to swear to his own innocence. Thus, ironically, his too-spirited champion darkened the last years of his life. It is even supposed that the affair hastened his death, which occurred in 1795.

In the meantime, Kotzebue had begun to be suspected. He squirmed, protested, told brazen lies, and wrote a canting letter to his mother which the harrassed lady had the misfortune to publish in a newspaper just at the time the true author was being unmasked. Legal proceedings against Kotzebue were set in motion; and the jester, famous or not, might have landed behind bars had he not taken flight home to Russian territory and the protection of Catherine II, who

[16] Kotzebue took the iron head from Bahrdt's "I am accustomed to butting at everything that stands in my way with an iron head." (Rieck 1966, p. 920). For Bahrdt and Kotzebue alike, this was an obvious take-off on the iron hand of history's and Goethe's Götz von Berlichingen, which "made mockery of Imperial authority" (*Götz*, I, 4.). The German *Union* is an allusion to the name of a group of free-thinkers who met in Bahrdt's tavern in Halle (Rabany 1893, p. 44 and Rieck 1966, pp. 929ff). That Kotzebue shared the non-political views of Bahrdt and company did not present an obstacle to his grasshopping mind.

had the inquiry quashed, probably (I surmise) out of friendship for Zimmermann. Kotzebue had intended nothing more with *Bahrdt* than fun for a day or a month, and no doubt he was stunned by the molehill's turning into a mountain that caved in on him. Once more he should have kept his mouth shut. In the late essay I have mentioned before, he retold the whole bitter story. If only he had not committed his "unverzeiliche Unbesonnenheit"—his unforgivable piece of recklessness—twenty-seven years before! He would have continued to be the critics' darling. But *Bahrdt* would hound him to his dying day. Goethe and Schiller had been granted quiet lives because they did not reply to their detractors. He should have kept quiet too. He was too sensitive. And he admonished his sons: "God give you the knack of keeping your tongues in your mouths."[17]

In 1794 he made a desperate attempt to staunch the wound by publishing, and distributing gratis to the public, a recantation and apology, invoking, among other things, his youthfulness at the time he had written *Bahrdt*. The youth (we note) had been twenty-nine years old. Still, it was an honest and manly apology. But the "better people" never forgave or forgot; his enemies never let go; he remained the blackguard who had crossed a certain unofficial line between permissible vituperation and dirty calumny.

Almost on the day Kotzebue received his own first copy of *Bahrdt*, his wife Friederike died in Weimar, at his mother's house, after giving birth to their fourth child. Kotzebue's grief was overwhelming and all his expressions of it sincere in my opinion, in spite of a theatricality that arouses suspicions in our century. But the episode also throws an arresting complementary light on Kotzebue. Unable to endure the spectacle of his wife's agony, he drove off to Paris, spent a month there taking in the sights of the Revolution, grieved over his loss, passed enjoyable evenings at the theaters, returned to Germany, and immediately published a book about everything he had done, felt, and seen. In it, wild *Sturm und Drang* mourning, informative comments on French playhouses and attacks on Jacobinism—Kotzebue truly hated cruelty— grotesquely amble arm-in-arm on the page, confirming and filling out our image of the man: flip, as I have said before, impulsive, warm, his heart on his sleeve, indefatigable, nervously galloping from one place and one emotion to the other, and apparently incapable of having a thought without at once sending it off to the printer. Perfectly aware, for the rest, of his heedlesness, humbled for a moment by his mother's dire shakings of the head, swearing after the *Bahrdt* affair never to play another vile trick, solemnly affirming that all he wanted was to live in peace with the whole world and cultivate his garden in Estonia, he was nevertheless in the end satisfied with himself and beyond mending.

---

[17] Kotzebue 1821, p. 103.

A convenient second chapter for a Life of Kotzebue might extend from the *Bahrdt* disaster to a national one: the collapse of Prussia in 1806.

Kotzebue's ingenuous account of his strange behavior at his wife's deathbed had set tongues wagging again, especially in Weimar, ever a focus for him of longing and anguish. The battered playwright retired for some five years to his peaceful estate of Friedenthal near what is today the town of Johvi in Estonia. With several children on his hands, and in spite of his numberless voyages a deep lover of domesticity, he remarried in 1794, choosing once again a noble heiress—a noble heiress in the German style, who spun and knitted, made gloves for her husband, and warbled, not bravura arias but pretty little songs. Now Kotzebue hunted, planted, scribbled to his heart's content, and in 1795 gladly gave up the magistracy he had so long neglected. In spite of his treatise *On the Aristocracy*, published in the midst of the *Bahrdt* scandal to curry Catherine's favor, the empress held our comedian in low regard, as we have seen, and suspected him of secret sympathies with Jacobinism. She dismissed Kotzebue from service with a small demotion in rank, but did him no further harm.

These were truly quiet and contented years for Kotzebue. Early in 1797 he received the visit of Stanislaus II, king of a Poland which had been partitioned out of existence in 1795. The King said to him, "You have made an epoch in dramatic literature. Many of your plays are translated into Polish, but I have also read the originals. You have converted our Polish ladies, who would only read French up to now. Were Frederick the Second still alive, your writings would have made him lose his hatred of the German language." Reporting this episode to his mother, Kotzebue added that he wished the critic of the *Allgemeine Literatur-Zeitung* (a newspaper which gave him no peace) had been present: he would have burst with anger. And he recommended that his mother say nothing about the visit, lest he be accused of boasting.[18]

Berlin in the meantime rejoiced in a new monarch, Frederic William III, as virtuous as his father had been dissolute. On January 2, 1798, Kotzebue's *Die silberne Hochzeit* (The Silver Wedding) was performed. The play exhibits a countess who rises to political eminence as a result of her high connections, commits all manner of mischief, is unmasked, and bundled off to jail. On January 3, on orders of the young king, Countess Lichtenau, his father's long-tenured mistress, was arrested. A lucky coincidence for Kotzebue, whose play was now given *very* particular applause.[19]

In the same year—the year, incidentally, in which a production of *Menschenhass und Reue* in London under the title *The Stranger* launched

---

[18] Mathes 1970, No. 25.
[19] Geiger 1895, pp. 181-182.

Kotzebue's plays on their conquest of the English and American theater[20] —he
was called to Vienna to become "secretary," but in effect director, of the two
Court theaters. He was by all accounts an effective and honest manager, but he
soon wearied of the conflicts and opposition his management provoked, and
secured his dismissal from the Emperor under highly favorable conditions,
including a pension, his nomination as Imperial Court Poet, and the lucrative
obligation of granting the Burgtheater first-production rights to all his plays—an
obligation which he faithfully carried out in later years. During his stay in
Vienna he wrote and produced one of his better comedies, and certainly his
most Viennese one, *Die beiden Klingsberg*—of which I have spoken already.
One of the editors of *Die deutschen Kleinstädter* writes that it was performed
one hundred and fifty times at the Burgtheater as late as in the 1950/1 season.[21]

It appears, however, that Kotzebue was still half-suspected of being a Jacobin, for many a jab at the aristocracy, the journey to Paris in 1790, and the
"immorality" of plays like *Bruder Moritz* and *La Peyrouse* kept the ludicrous
accusation alive. The Austrian secret police shadowed him for three months.
At one point a newspaper in Gotha even published a report that he had been
arrested for spreading democratic ideas. Vienna, it must be added, was and long
remained strung in the noose of official censorship, in contrast to the remarkable
freedom of expression allowed in Berlin by the new king. Besides all this,
Kotzebue's wife thoroughly disliked the Austrian capital—we are not told why.
Altogether, he was ready to install the family for a year or two in Weimar, after
a long absence from his birthplace.

It goes without saying that all this time Kotzebue was steadily writing and
publishing. I will mention here only a volume of four plays printed in 1798—
his *Neue Schauspiele*—because, following a fulsome dedication to King Stanislaus, it contains a declaration of principles which is strongly reminiscent of
Lope de Vega's defiant *Arte nuevo de hacer comedias en este tiempo* (The New
Art of Writing Plays in These Times, 1609), a Horatian poem the Spaniard
mirthfully delivered to the Academy of Madrid. I give a few of Lope's lines in
prose:

[20] It was Sheridan who produced the play at Drury Lane with John Kemble and Mrs. Siddons in the
starring roles. It opened to a packed house, enjoyed 26 repeat performances that season, and was
selected to introduce the winter season in the same year. Until 1842 not a year went by without a
production of *The Stranger*. Productions tapered off thereafter, but it seems that the play was re-
vived intermittently in London until 1872. It might be noted here that the English *reading* public got
its first Kotzebue play two years earlier—in 1796—when a translation of his *Negersklaven* (The
Negro Slaves) appeared in print, hot from its appearance in Germany, for the topic of slavery was
much on people's minds, from the House of Lords to the Evangelicals. See Sellier 1901, *passim.*

[21] Nedde 1978, p. 84. I am poorly informed about the performance history of Kotzebue's plays in
Germany and Austria. While substantial monographs treat performance history in English-speaking
countries, Spain, Norway, and Russia, no comprehensive work on this subject exists for Germany
and Austria—another indication, no doubt, of the pervasive hostility to Kotzebue. Nor is there, to
my knowledge, a yearly index to current productions in the German world. The *Chronik und Bilanz
eines Bühnenjahres*, despite its promising title, is not helpful in this respect.

I can't call anyone more barbarous than myself, since I dare give precepts against [high] art, and allow myself to be carried along by the popular current; whence they call me an ignoramus in Italy and France. But what can I do—having written 483 plays, including one that I finished this week, and all but six of them sinning grievously against high art? When all is said and done I defend what I have written and recognize that while my plays might have been of better quality, they would not have had the success they have enjoyed had I written them otherwise. For sometimes that which is incorrect [*contro el justo*] gives delight for that very reason.

And now Kotzebue:

I have little to say about this collection of my new plays. As they have had the good fortune to please the public, they will undoubtedly displease the critics. The bitter, scornful judgments; the contempt for public applause; the rude, arrogant manner of writing about my works, and sometimes about my person; the malicious innuendos concerning the morality of my plays; the obvious effort carefully to pick out every weak spot and even more carefully to veil what is good in them; all this I have grown so accustomed to that I need not waste words over it.

I know better than any critic that I do not write masterpieces, and that my proper place is that of a second-rank writer. The main purpose of my works is to be effective on stage. This purpose they achieve in fact, and this is the point of view from which they ought to be judged. But this is just what people will not do. Well, let them fare on in God's name and abuse me as before. I hope that the public, which has done me justice these many years, will continue to provide me with balm against these mosquito-bites.

True, the sincerity of such disclaimers is always questionable. Kotzebue did not like to hear from others what he himself was willing to say about his work. But a partial honesty has to be granted to this and quite a few other remarks after the same fashion he let fall throughout his career.[22] Kotzebue exemplifies the in-between artist, who is neither a "commercial hack" nor a member of the artistic elite. The hack practices his craft in his own happy world as if he simply belonged to another profession or guild. But the in-betweener never stops longing for a place among the Goethes and Schillers—whoever they may be in his time and place. Ten thousand spectators applaud him; but full of anguish he listens for, and does not hear, the applause of the ten. To conceal his anguish he

---

[22] See his *Fragmente über Recensenten-Unfug* (Fragments of Critics' Mischief, 1797); a comment, preserved in his posthumous papers, to the effect that his plays, unlike his historical works, had cost him little effort to write; and various light-hearted remarks concerning the public's limited intellectual capacities.

denies that he has any ambition to please these terrible ten. And to some extent this is true. And to some grievous extent it is not true. All his life Kotzebue remained obsessed with Weimar, and Weimar meant, not his mother, whom he would have loved as well anywhere else, but the Intellectual Elite. What they will say of me in Weimar, or This will show them in Weimar—cries of this kind recur in the surviving documents with almost pathetic frequency.

The year is 1799. Content on the whole with his brief span in Vienna, Kotzebue toured southern Germany with his family during the summer, and in the fall returned to Weimar as if to try again. His complacent self-justifications suggest that *Bahrdt* has become a dimming memory—for him. He was a great man in the world and not about to enter Weimar humbly riding an ass. The ass figures in another comedy: *Der hyperboräische Esel, oder die heutige Bildung* (The Hyperborean Ass, or Education Today, 1799), in which he took on the Romantic "heads in the clouds" in general and the Schlegel brothers, apostles of Romanticism, in particular.[23] With his customary flippancy he attacked F. Schlegel's novel *Lucinde* for its immorality as if he himself had never been taxed with his forgiven adulteresses, embraced illegitimate offsprings, flirtations with incest, and other titillating breaches of propriety. Perhaps he realized that the deeply serious voluptuous enthusiasm of *Lucinde* carried readers a world away from the sentimental or comic thinness of his own audacities.

Before this new literary quarrel could peak, Kotzebue, taking his family back to Estonia for a visit, was arrested at the Russian border by the police of Catherine's successor, the maniacal Paul I, for whom every foreigner crossing the border was a probable Jacobin. Dumbfounded, separated from his wife and children who were left unmolested, Kotzebue was dragged away to Siberia. His account of this experience, translated into English in 1802 as *The Most Memorable Year in the Life of August von Kotzebue*, is well worth reading again after nearly two centuries. The book is devoid of posturing and heroics—in spite of an almost comical attempt Kotzebue made to escape en route; and a prisoner who describes his tears, his terrors, his abjectly submissive epistles to the monster who has condemned him earns, at any rate, our belief in his veracity. Kotzebue had the means to be driven to his exile in a carriage, but he saw and commiserated with the wretches who had to walk in chains to the Urals and beyond. In remote Tobolsk, the governor courteously but helplessly received him. His plays had been performed there; everybody knew him. In the primitive village of Kurgan, to which he was assigned, the rustic folk were not familiar with his plays, but they were mightily impressed when someone, opening a

[23] The stormy relations between Kotzebue on one side and Goethe or the Romantics on the other have been described and analyzed more times than is perhaps necessary. The definitive and exhaustive study is that of F. Stock, 1971. Dissertations by Ida Wohlmuth (Vienna 1925) and J. Kotzur (Breslau 1932) are also useful, as is the relevant chapter in Rabany's Life. Nothing exists in English. For full documentation concerning titles before Stock, see Goedeke 1964.

Moscow newspaper, read in it an article concerning Kotzebue's fame in England.

Kotzebue had left Weimar on April 10, 1800. On July 7, without explanation, he got news in Kurgan that the Tsar had pardoned him, no one knew for what, and given him permission to rejoin his family. Arriving in the Ural community of Niznij Tagil (as it is called today), long-bearded and in rags—looking, he says, like poor Tom in *King Lear*—and devouring his bread and cheese, he was suddenly surrounded by an elegant crowd of Russians and Germans "of the first rank" eager to meet and greet the famous personage.

In St. Petersburg the Tsar made much of him, rewarded him with yet another estate in Livonia (along with its serfs) and all but forced him to become the director of the resident German Court Theater. No one dared cross the impossible monarch. Kotzebue trembled lest a word dropped by an actor in a play send him back to Kurgan. The very word "republic" was forbidden. "Fatherland" had to be changed to plain "land." A character was not allowed to have come from Paris. And a line reading "I'm going to Russia; it's good and cold over there" had to be rewritten as "I'm going to Russia; it's full of honest people." The Censor himself trembled. Kotzebue found himself a favorite terrified by the favor. He had just been ordered to write a description of one of the Tsar's palaces when the monarch was assassinated, to everyone's relief. Soon after, his son and heir Alexander I gave Kotzebue and his family permission to leave the country. It should be taken for granted by now that one of Kotzebue's first acts (so to speak) was to make a book out of his adventures.

This strange interruption behind him, Kotzebue was ready again for Weimar and its more congenial battles. This is the period in which our comedy was written and produced. It is a brief one, extending from the middle of the year 1801 to the middle of 1802, with a break for a most flattering distinction. A new theater had been built in Berlin. Its director, A. M. Iffland (himself the writer of many a moral and larmoyant bourgeois drama), invited Kotzebue to write a play for the opening of the house on the first of January 1802. Kotzebue complied; and the Royal Theater[24] was inaugurated with his *Die Kreuzfahrer* (The Crusaders, 1802), the author himself attending, of course. Indeed, Kotzebue contributed to the very next show as well, adapting a libretto from the French for a "magic opera" by G. F. Reichardt.

As always, Berlin was kind, Weimar exasperating. For A. W. Schlegel had greeted Kotzebue on his return from exile with a volley of printed insults bearing the sarcastic title *Honor Portal and Triumphal Arch for the Theater-President von Kotzebue on the Occasion of his Hoped-for Return to the Fatherland*. The "President" in this title was a gibe aimed at Kotzebue's judicial title. Schlegel opened his barrage against Kotzebue with ten satirical sonnets. "You,

[24] The term "National Theater" smacked of the French Revolution and was out.

apostle from England to Hesperia," the first of them began—an acknowledgment, after all, of Kotzebue's unparalleled successes in Europe. The second sonnet, translated into English by the author himself as the third of the series, devoted itself entirely to Kotzebue's acclaim among the English:

> He still does cheer your porter-thickened blood,

went one of its heavy lines. The other sonnets belabored their victim for his venal sentimentality. I note again that Schlegel had nothing to say about Kotzebue's comic work. The world loved or despised him as a maker of Elevated Drama.

After the sonnets, Schlegel introduced a series of epigrams, one each for Kotzebue's "noble" plays to date: he had read them all, it seems. But the bulk of the *Trimphal Arch* consists of a rather funny play entitled *The Liberation of Kotzebue, or the Virtuous Exile*, denominated "a sentimental-romantic play in two acts." Here, again and again, we are reminded by Schlegel himself of Kotzebue's amazing popularity: "German theater and Kotzebue are practically one and the same," says the prompter in Act One.

The amusing premise is that Kotzebue has gone to Russia to find a new subject for a play. The Tsar, however, has read *Doctor Bahrdt*. Indignant at so much vileness, he has had Kotzebue arrested and sent to Siberia. Kotzebue's characters, led by La Peyrouse, gather to liberate their creator. Schlegel's wit soon falters, however, and by the time we reach the epilogue's refrain,

> Nun willkommen, Liebster, du
> Kotzebue! Kotzebue!
> Bubu—bubu—bubu—bu!

our patience with literary squabbles may have worn thin. The long little play is followed by a poem in *terza rima*, entitled "Kotzebue's Description of his Journey," which Kotzebue may have mistaken for the triolets he brings up in connection with Schlegel's sonnets in the fifth act of *Die deutschen Kleinstädter*.

Presently our hero's relations with Goethe deteriorated too. Goethe was at that time the revered friend of the Romantics, and while he certainly did not identify himself with them, he was not about to make enemies of them for Kotzebue's sake. Hearing of the latter's kind reception by Paul I, he had, in a letter, snippily expressed his hope that the Tsar would keep the playwright in the Russian capital. When Kotzebue installed himself in Weimar (and in a summer house in nearby Jena), Goethe pointedly failed to invite him to his choice Wednesday gatherings. Kotzebue countered with his own lively Thursdays. Nevertheless, in early 1802 he handed Goethe the manuscript of his new comedy; a routine action, since Goethe, like every other theatrical director, relied on the popular author for a considerable fraction of his repertory. The

Weimar premiere was set for the end of February. But after examining the play, Goethe decided to strike all the satirical references to Schlegel and his own brother-in-law Vulpius. He did not object to a little banter with his poem *Das Veilchen*, but he claimed that he wanted no topical literary quarrels on his stage. Kotzebue was indignant. Words passed between the two men. Kotzebue's wife urged her husband never again to show his plays at Weimar, and his mother meddled, this time irritating both Goethe and her son.[25] It so happened that at this very time Kotzebue was trying to organize a celebration in Jena for Schiller's birthday, which fell on the fifth of March. Was this fussing over Schiller meant to draw the poet into the squabble on his side? Perhaps; because it appears that Kotzebue now appealed to him to raise his voice against Goethe's excisions. The appeal itself does not survive, but we do have Schiller's reply of March 2, 1802.[26] It is a model of epistolary diplomacy. Schiller has borrowed the censored script from Goethe, as requested by Kotzebue. "After a careful reading of the play I can find nothing arbitrary in his way of proceeding; he has crossed out no other passages except such as could excite the party-spirit he wants to banish from the theater." He goes on to remark that the deletions do not affect either the action or the character-portrayals, and he assures Kotzebue that even though some people may want to create strife between Kotzebue and himself because the verses concluding the third act might be in part aimed at himself, he will not allow this to happen. Even if these lines were in fact pointed at him, he would not mind, "for comedy is very free, and a merry spirit [*die gute, heitre Laune*] is allowed to go quite far; only passion must be excluded." In conclusion, he advises Kotzebue to give in; giving in will redound to his honor.[27]

Kotzebue did not heed Schiller's advice, perhaps because by that time the elaborate Schiller-celebration he had concocted had disintegrated. Once more he saw Goethe's hand behind the mishap—unjustly, it seems. He now withdrew his play altogether from Goethe, and its premiere took place at the Burgtheater in Vienna on March 22. Kotzebue lingered in Weimar long enough to stage a private performance for his friends—on June 3, 1802—with himself in the role

[25] See the excellent accounts of these events in Stock 1971, pp. 34-36, and Mathes 1972, pp. 578-591, where the censored passages and the feeble replacements suggested by Goethe are reprinted. I give a few more details in the notes to my translation *infra*.

[26] The letter is undated, but its date was conclusively determined by R. Schlösser in 1903 in a brief, precise, but typically hostile article in which Kotzebue is treated as a cunning and contemptible *Intrigant*.

[27] This letter was first printed—with a typographical error—in Kotzebue 1821, pp. 361-362. It is still a mystery in what way the verses in question could be thought to be directed against Schiller. Schlösser's antipathy goes so far that, without being able to answer this question, he elaborates a convoluted hypothesis to blacken Kotzebue. The latter, he suggests, knew that Goethe had left this passage uncensored, and believed that when Schiller realized this, he would conclude that Goethe, after deleting unfriendly allusions to the Schlegels, had purposely let stand an insult to Schiller! Surely a more serene hypothesis is that after a hasty reading, Schiller confused these verses (III, 14) with the allusion to his famous "Ode to Joy" (III, 4).

of Sperling the fool.

Goethe remained even-keeled then and later; he *could* not allow a gadfly like Kotzebue to move him. As soon as plays were printed, authors lost their rights in them. *Die deutschen Kleinstädter* was published at the end of 1802, and in November 1803 Goethe staged it at Weimar, presumably as cut by himself. Furthermore, he continued to draw on Kotzebue's work, comic or serious, to please the public and make money for the playhouse. Out of a total of 4809 performances given during his twenty-six years at the helm, 667 were of 87 plays by Kotzebue, by far the highest number for any author.[28] Personally Goethe wanted nothing to do with Kotzebue, but in his lifelong preoccupation with the fertile playwright as a man of letters and a man of the theater he exhibits an alternation of praise and contempt which is evidence of repeated attempts to come to a fair summation.[29] On his death-bed he asked for a script he had been working on: it was a revision of yet another Kotzebue play. . . .

Weimar had once again become uncomfortable for Kotzebue. The rights and the wrongs in these infinite squabbles, slights, resentments, and misunderstandings formed by this time an unclarifiable tangle. But the Goethe party had roots and volume; Kotzebue was a fly-by. In a staring contest, it was he, inevitably, who would be the first to lower his eyes. Fortunately for him, there was always friendly Berlin; and there he set himself down with his family toward the end of the year 1802. Presently he became the editor of a journal called *Der Freimütige* (the word means "frank," "outspoken") where he wasted no time laying the whole *Kleinstädter* row before the public. "Far be it from me," he remarked, "to belittle the beloved Goethe who created 'Iphigenia' and 'Tasso,' but I cannot honor Goethe the despot of taste."[30]

The magazine was a success. Kotzebue boasted that the king himself was one of its anonymous contributors. He was certainly one of its readers, as were the rulers of Austria and Russia. Kotzebue, who was a first-rate journalist, did not weary his public with incessant attacks on Goethe and his other foes. He printed a wealth of information on matters political, literary, artistic, theological and philosophical, economic, and scientific. A general approach of enlightened tolerance included, typically, a favorable view of the Jews—the kind of welcome which many Romantics and nationalists were presently to withdraw. In short, Kotzebue remained true to his eighteenth-century self.[31]

As I have noted, the first production of *Die deutschen Kleinstädter* took place in Vienna in March of 1802. In April it was performed in Hamburg and then in Berlin. One of the reviewers there was none other than A. W. Schlegel who, writing in the *Zeitung für die elegante Welt*, called the play a farce, spoke at

[28] Klingenberg 1962, p. 17, et al.
[29] The best account is in Stock 1971, pp. 36-43.
[30] Nedden 1978, p. 85.
[31] Geiger 1895, p. 152.

length of its triteness, admitted that a few of its episodes were merry, and suggested that *this* sort of thing was at any rate better than Kotzebue's melodramas. I have already mentioned Kotzebue's reply in the same journal to the effect that he would *not* reply as long as he knew that his critic was incapable of writing as good a comedy as his.[32]

Not replying was, in any event, a thing unnatural for Kotzebue, and it may be around this time that he wrote a witless and scurrilous playlet, *Expectorationem: a Work of Art, also a Prologue to Alarcos*, published in 1803 but understandably excluded, along with the Bahrdt scribble, from collected editions of his works. Here, in Bahrdic style, he punched away at the Schlegels once more, and at Goethe of course—in general for the latter's Olympian monopolizing of worship, and in particular for his censorship of *Die deutschen Kleinstädter*.[33] In the course of this unsavory little text, the Schlegels (called Mister Rage and Mister Rave) lick up Goethe's spittle, bemoan Kotzebue's successes and the critical thrashings they suffer at his hands, beg Goethe to whip Kotzebue back to Siberia before they burst with envy, and request his protection for *Alarcos*, here called *Infarctus*. Despite their intimation that Goethe has outlived his genius, the master, falling asleep under the fumes of their incense, dreams that he has become the Pope, while the two lickspittles set his snores to music.

Die deutschen Kleinstädter did not achieve the sensational popularity and fame of *Menschenhass*—nothing of his ever did again—but 18 performances in Weimar until 1817,[34] 130 performances in Vienna, and 129 in Berlin from 1802 to 1855[35] translate to a very handsome showing. The assumption must be that it fared well in other cities too. It was performed "with great success" by the German players of St. Petersburg in 1804 and remained a favorite there.[36] That it influenced Gogol's *Revisor* (The Inspector-General, 1836) admits of no doubt. In France, where a translation appeared in 1841,[37] it enjoyed the curious favor of becoming a standard German textbook well into our century. A couple of editions published in England suggest that there too it may have been used in some schoolrooms. But as no English translation was made of it, Kotzebue's best work remained for all practical purposes unknown in the Anglo-Saxon world.

[32] Stock 1971, p. 170, and Mathes 1972, p. 590.

[33] *Expectorare*: to banish scornfully from one's mind; but I am unable to account for the noun form in the accusative. For "A Work of Art," see note 21 to the fourth act of *The Good Citizens of Piffelheim. Alarcos* was F. Schlegel's failed drama, rejected for the opening of the new Berlin theater in 1802 in favor of Kotzebue's *Crusaders*. As for Goethe's vanity, Kotzebue was hardly the only person aware of it. Even the admiring Madame de Staël spoke of his "amour-propre d'une nature aussi bizarre que son imagination. Il se croit inspiré d'une manière surnaturelle" (Staël 1982, p. 215).

[34] Bürkhardt 1891, *passim.*

[35] Mathes 1972, p. 589.

[36] Giesemann 1971, p. 175.

[37] Thompson 1928, p. 153.

Although Kotzebue himself does not take special notice of *Die deutschen Kleinstädter* in his later writings, he must have been confident of public familiarity with it, since he re-used the name of his little town in two more plays: *Carolus Magnus* (1806), another one of his almost-wonderful comedies, and again in the insignificant *Des Esels Schatten, oder der Prozess in Krähwinkel* (The Ass's Shadow, or the Lawsuit in Krähwinkel, 1810). For more evidence of survival, we note that Johann Nestroy exploited the name for his fire-brand *Freiheit in Krähwinkel* (Freedom in Krähwinkel, 1848); and although Kotzebue had not invented the name—it occurs in Old High German[38] —his little masterpiece turned it into a standard entry in the dictionaries.

While yet in Weimar, Kotzebue had written and staged a couple of dramatic skits which he now printed as part of a new venture he proposed to his publisher Kummer—for whom one more grand idea from Kotzebue was all in the day's business. This one was to bring out once a year an almanac of intimate and easily staged works for amateurs. The idea had come to Kotzebue from certain French models—his political enmity to Jacobins and "Buonaparte" never prevented him from raiding the French for literary booty—and from 1803 to the end of his life he never failed to produce an *Almanach dramatischer Spiele*, each one containing a bundle of plays, some sweet and tearful, some merry, some mildly salacious—here in prose, there in his sprightly verse. The reader will remember that they have yielded most of the titles for my imaginary *Selected Comedies by Kotzebue*.

Within a year of his settlement in Berlin—in August 1803—Kotzebue's second wife died. Once again the widower journeyed to Paris in order to distract himself, remained a few months, and returned to marry his third and last wife (who survived him until 1852) and—of course—to write an account of his stay in the French capital.

The *Erinnerungen aus Paris im Jahre 1804* (promptly translated into English under the title *Travels from Berlin, through Switzerland, to Paris in the Year 1804*), although in no way "profound," is as fascinating in its way as the story of his exile to Siberia. At the beginning, the book addresses a certain "dear friend," who, it is easy to guess, is his late wife's cousin, the lady he will marry on his return—apparently with the blessing of the dying woman. This time Kotzebue spares the reader the tearful ravings he had inflicted on him in his first book—whether because his taste had improved or his sorrow was smaller is impossible to tell. The peace between Prussia and Russia on one side and France on the other still held, so that Kotzebue could enjoy himself without derogating from his loyalty to Berlin and St. Petersburg. He was in fact received with every mark of respect as an eminent writer and a member of the Russian nobility of the robe. Kotzebue writes with unaffected modesty, but

---

[38] *Chrawinchil*: a backwater town where the crows go to roost; Putz 1977.

gladly reports on the plays by his hand being performed and discussed in Paris. *Menschenhass* was still in the forefront, but another success was his *Die Versöhnung, oder Bruderzwist* (The Reconciliation, or Fraternal Strife, 1798), translated as *Les deux frères*. He speaks of the courtesies extended to him wherever he went, of theatrical life and manners in Paris, of his meeting with Picard, the man who had inspired *Die deutschen Kleinstädter* and was now running the Théatre Louvois, and points out that the lady who has translated *Menschenhass* into French has made a fortune, while he, the author, has earned from it a mere 200 taler, just enough to live on in misery for a year. He meets with Bonaparte (who is still First Consul, though about to crown himself Emperor) at the theater where *Les deux frères* is being shown, and has a lively professional talk with the dictator, who, he notes, is putting on weight. He sees him a second time at an audience in the Tuileries, where he is also invited to a grand, formal dinner. He makes the acquaintance of the two other consuls, of Monsieur Guillotin, and of Madame Récamier, whose intimate he quickly becomes. He tells the French the "truth" about Weimar and disillusions his hearers concerning this so-called paradise of the Muses. Characteristically, he prefers the classicizing Saint-Sulpice to the medieval Notre-Dame, and admires the paintings of David and Gérard—the latter the portraitist of Frederick William III. Always humane, he admires the excellent charitable institutions, the fair judicial proceedings, the pensions for superannuated players and the society for the protection of authors' rights, and, touring the museums, expresses his dislike of Descents of the Cross and scenes of martyrs being roasted, impaled, or flayed. He is happy to report that everyone is heartily sick of the revolution. He tremulously hopes that peace will endure. He is shocked by the free behavior of French women and by the willingness of audiences to submit to the fecal matter of Molière's *Physician in Spite of Himself* (duly forgetting his own scatological passages in *Bahrdt*). But he is deeply disturbed by the censorship Bonaparte has imposed on the French, and concludes his otherwise extremely friendly book with the remark that in France one can publish anything one likes against Christianity; but against . . . beware! Cayenne![39]

After his marriage to Wilhelmine Friederike von Kursell in August 1804, Kotzebue took his wife on a honeymoon tour to Italy, travelling as far as Naples. A few months later, back in Berlin, he had, inevitably, another book to offer the public, one even bulkier than his recent Parisian volume. One hardly knows how the man found time both to have and to record his experiences, but somehow he always did; and the result is once again eminently readable. A four-volume English edition soon appeared on the market. To the extent that the book is a conscientious cicerone, detailing the contents of palaces, churches, and museums, it may at best retain some marginal interest for art historians; but

[39] The penal colony in French Guyana.

were these sections to be excised in a new edition (as would be easy to do), the remainder, consisting of Kotzebue's fresh, irreverent, and very personal observations of life and manners—especially in Naples—might interest readers as much today as they did in Kotzebue's time. As usual, he is incapable of seeking out fundamental causes or imagining explanations other than would come to the mind of a brisk journalist—but he is a pungent observer, a benevolent skeptic, always his own man—not overawed by Classics—and refreshingly willing to say that he hated the whole business—the poverty, the dirt, the hunger, the thievery, the ignorance. Everywhere he noted French plunder of art treasures. He disliked Bernini, whose fountain in the Piazza Navona seemed ridiculous to him, and dismissed as meaningless the obelisks the Popes had put up everywhere in Rome—perhaps not so foolish an opinion, after all. As was to be expected, he fell in with several productions of his plays, one of them transmogrified into a ballet. In Naples he discovered that the public laughed at *Menschenhass* instead of crying; a bit of marital infidelity simply amused them. He found libraries deserted, gambling obsessive, the smell of defecation everywhere and overwhelming, and beggars, beggars on every side. One day, walking in the street, he watched in horror a woman sink to the pavement and literally die of hunger before an indifferent crowd inured to scenes of this kind. Seeing the Tyrol again on his return, he could not find words enough to express his happiness and admiration. And then Berlin:

> I approached Berlin with a beating heart; with a happy spirit I saw once more the towers of the capital of a land which, although it has no oranges for the palate, allows the tongue to speak, and the brain to think, without poisoning every word through a spy and every thought through a censor. Here, where confidence in the government is allied to genuine enlightenment; here, where true freedom reigns; where the citizen obeys wise laws, not whims, laws which make him the nobleman's equal—the only *rational* equality!—here I hang up my pilgrim's staff, as an *ex voto*, in the Temple of the Muses, far from that of Bellona.[40]

Words dictated in part, perhaps, by a conscious sense of where his self-interest lay; but at the same time clearly sprung from the heart.

As for his joy at being far from Bellona, the truth is that there was nothing warlike about Kotzebue. His pugnacity was entirely literary and distinctly more an effect of general exuberance than an expression of malevolence. He readily forgave, and, more significant, readily asked for forgiveness, and seems never to have dreamed of intriguing against the foes he peppered or doing them any harm other than assailing them in a farce or a pamphlet. Unfortunately for him, his

[40] Kotzebue 1842-1843, pp. 323-324.

modesty, humanity, and good humor lacked the noise-making power of his literary quarrels and indiscretions.

The French had honored Kotzebue with membership in the Société des Observateurs de l'Homme. Back in Berlin, he was named to the Prussian Academy of Science, and the King made available to him a mass of unpublished historical documents in the archives of Königsberg. It should be kept in mind that, for all the claptrap that mars his ambitious drama, Kotzebue had read a great deal of history for much of his work. Like Schiller, then, he felt strongly attracted to historical research; and by 1805 he had begun to labor in earnest on a Prussian history based on the fresh materials placed at his disposal.

In the same period, he was also appointed canon to the cathedral of Magdeburg—an indication, no doubt, of the contempt in which the Church was held by the Protestant elite. It goes without saying that he continued to enjoy his Russian title, incomes, citizenship, and estates.[41] But he had every reason to remain in Berlin. An unfriendly writer records that he was "the oracle of the Queen's tea".[42] He appeared as one of the two thousand choice guests invited to attend and participate in a brilliant birthday celebration for the latter at which no fewer than eighty members of the royal circle were present. Dawn was near when, in one of the quadrilles, our Kotzebue danced in dressed as a priest of Mercury, a crown of poppies on his head and a caduceus in his hand, looking so ugly and ungraceful, reports Madame de Staël, that she feared her imagination was poisoned for life. Incidentally, the Frenchwoman—who was "conquering" Berlin after having swept up Weimar—slyly invited both A. W. Schlegel and Kotzebue to one of her gatherings, pretending to be unaware of literary quarrels. The result remains unknown to us.[43]

But Kotzebue was destined never to stay long in one place. In December 1804 the First Consul had crowned himself Emperor at Notre-Dame. Soon afterward, the third coalition was formed to do battle with the French. In November 1805 Napoleon occupied Vienna. A month later he crushed the Russian and Austrian armies at Austerlitz. Still Prussia kept aloof. Indeed, now that the Habsburg monarch had lost his title of emperor and was reduced to a mere king, there was even talk that Napoleon might allow Frederick William to become emperor of Prussia. But the Prussians soon found cause for distrusting the French dictator. Frederick William, who had long been blamed by an influential war party for his policy of neutrality, allied himself belatedly with the Tsar, declared war on the French, and saw his armies humiliatingly overwhelmed at Jena and Auerstedt. Bellona had come to Prussia after all. On

---

[41] "I cannot deny that my vanity has sometimes been tickled by the thought that I am the only German writer who has been pensioned by three great Courts (those of Russia, Prussia and Austria)." Kotzebue 1922, p. 190.

[42] Letter by the publisher Karl Bertuch, in Mathes 1972, p. 583.

[43] Staël 1982, pp. 275 and 277. It may be surmised that her catty remark about Kotzebue's appearance was meant to please Goethe.

October 27, 1806, Napoleon entered Berlin. The Court fled east, and so did Kotzebue, who took his family to the relative safety of Estonia, where he purchased a new estate and resumed the rural life which had always been to his taste.

The third chapter of Kotzebue's life begins peacefully at Schwarzen, his new property—the French were to leave this corner of Europe unmolested—and concludes with his death at Mannheim in 1819.

Busy as ever with his plays and with his history of ancient Prussia, Kotzebue now put his journalistic experiences to a new use: political pamphleteering against the invader of Prussia. Swept away were the amiable feelings so recently vented in his Parisian reminiscences. In three successive periodicals, between the years 1808 and 1815, he rushed, pen in hand, to the defense of his three grand patrons, the rulers of Russia, Prussia, and Austria. Buonaparte (as Kotzebue and the Emperor's other enemies called him) was well aware of these activities. In 1810, during an interval of peace, he made Alexander suppress the first of Kotzebue's periodicals, called *The Bee*. Thereupon Kotzebue launched a second one bearing for its title a new metaphor, *The Cricket*. In one issue of Napoleon's *Le Moniteur*, Kotzebue was flatteringly damned together with Baron Stein (the great Prussian minister) and the Cossacks. As far as I know, these journalistic pieces have not been studied or anthologized. I have read a few of them—enough to admire their verve, their eloquence, the voluble persiflage, the strong sense for striking details. Be that as it may, they contributed to the award of the Order of St. Ann, Second Class, which Alexander bestowed on Kotzebue in 1815.

I have mentioned already that Kotzebue had become a member of learned academies in Paris and Berlin. Learned institutions in Antwerp and St. Petersburg also admitted him, and the philosophy faculty of Königsberg granted him its doctorate. It seems strange, perhaps, to think of Kotzebue as a scholar, but his *Preussens ältere Geschichte* (The History of Ancient Prussia, 1809) was received by professional historians with marks of sincere respect; and there is no doubt that Kotzebue took his work seriously and loved it. Writing plays, he said, came ever so easily to him. This, instead, was hard work and the matter was solid.

The letter he wrote in 1810 describing his life as landowner on his Baltic estate should be recalled at this juncture (see pages 54-55). We must picture Kotzebue surrounded by an affectionate family, looking after his farmlands, hunting—presumably with other landowners of the area—and then for long hours working now on some dramatic trifle, now on another anti-French pamphlet, now on some medieval Prussian document. It is a pity that so few letters and other source-materials are available to furnish out the picture; but one letter which is preserved cannot fail to interest us, since it comes from Beethoven. Kotzebue, many of whose plays are in effect attractive libretti for eventual composers, had provided Beethoven with the texts for *King Stephen* and *The Ruins of Athens*, both composed in 1811. (The latter, by the way, is a handsome compliment not only to the Habsburg monarch, but also to Schiller and even Goethe.) In January 1812, the composer courteously requested "an opera from your unique dramatic genius, whether it be romantic, perfectly serious, heroic, comical, or sentimental—in short, I will gladly accept whatever you offer," although he suggested a preference for the "darker ages," perhaps something about Attila.[44] Unfortunately, the reply to this letter has not survived.

When Napoleon began his push into Russia in 1812, Kotzebue fled with his family to St. Petersburg, ready to continue to Sweden if necessary. His eldest son, an officer in the Russian army, fell on the battlefield. In 1813, in the wake of the Napoleonic retreat, the Russians entered Berlin in friendly triumph. Kotzebue was named Consul-General in Königsberg, with the special assignments of keeping watch over public opinion and impeding contraband to Russia. He had hoped that this post would be a sinecure, and may have remembered the easy days as magistrate in Reval. Instead, his obligations were burdensome and time-consuming. True, he continued to publish political pamphlets, histories,[45] plays, and even a report on the manufactures of Russia, but he did not care for the long hours spent issuing documents or sending Cossacks after smugglers. In 1816 he was unexpectedly relieved of his duties—without prejudice, he writes, and to his great satisfaction. Whatever the reasons may have been, Kotzebue soon came up with another one of his innumerable ideas. "The Court," he told the Tsar in a memorandum, "sends travelers abroad so they can look at factories, new machinery and the like, describe them, and make them useful to Russia. Will it not be equally, or even more advantageous, if the Court keeps a man abroad who can inform it of all the new ideas concerning politics, economics, warfare, public education etc. which are gaining currency in Europe—a man who will furnish short extracts and allow Russia to avail itself of ideas which are the precious property of foreign nations?" Continuing, he pointed out that, inasmuch as the Russian censor allowed few foreign books into the country, there really was no other way of importing fresh ideas. Furthermore, he would be performing the self-same task which Baron Grimm had undertaken many years before on behalf of the Empress Catherine.[46]

The Russian authorities must have realized that Kotzebue was perfectly qualified for this congenial compilatory work. His proposal was accepted, and Alexander sent him off with the title of Councillor of State, and such

---

[44] W. von Kotzebue 1881, p. 150. A brief letter from Haydn, written in 1802, also survives. In it, the seventy-year-old composer courteously turns down some request for a collaboration which Kotzebue must have sent him.

[45] After the history of Prussia already mentioned, Kotzebue published a *History of Ludwig IV* (Emperor from 1328 to 1347); a *History of the German Reich*; and (posthumously) *Contributions to the History of Lithuania, Russia, Poland, and Prussia*.

[46] Kotzebue 1922, pp. 207-208.

encomiums that Kotzebue was ashamed to write them down. In the spring of 1817 he left Russia once more and took up residence, as will be guessed, in Weimar, near his aging mother, and with high hopes for the future.

In 1809 he had written to Kummer that thenceforth he would compose nothing but comedies.[47] This was hyperbole, but most of his later dramatic works are in fact comic: Kotzebue had achieved artistic self-knowledge. The best of these is the comedy of *Der Rehbock* (The Roebuck), produced in Berlin, Weimar, and Vienna in 1814/1815. Deeply indebted (as often before) to Marivaux, but also to the much "naughtier" playwrights of the Dancourt type, Kotzebue's play is too complicated and sometimes too strained to be a complete success. But his contemporaries were too shocked by its immorality to reason over fine points of aesthetics. Once again Kotzebue proved to be too Gallic for the Germanic world. And yet the Voltairean spirit deserted him once it came to defending himself. He could not deny that his play toyed with, and went to the fringe of, some very ticklish sexual situations, but instead of attacking his contemporaries for their stuffiness and hypocrisy, he took his usual stand, intellectually docile but rhetorically aggressive, prepared a declaration (which he did not live to publish) to the effect that his play was in fact perfectly moral, since no one in it literally and positively committed the sin he or she was tempted to indulge in. Besides, he argued, innocent maidens would not understand the equivocal allusions. And what about Goethe? Foul language in *Faust*; two wives in *Stella*; a "glaring love affair" in *Götz*; an uncondemned suicide in *Werther*—yet no one ever blamed Goethe![48] In any event, the press and other enemies would hardly have accepted his defence; they never had before. One critic suggested that women should be denied entrance to the theater for this play. Taken to a performance after Kotzebue's death, Felix Mendelssohn called it "the most infamous, reprehensible, wretched thing the late Kotzebue ever created" and could not forgive the friend who had invited him for enjoying it.[49] Goethe, however—who never lost his equanimity vis-à-vis the quicksilver author—thoroughly enjoyed the play's frivolities. Kotzebue's mother reported in a letter to her son, "Goethe likes The Roebuck very much; he thinks it is one of your best comedies. He has attended all the rehearsals and has almost died laughing. He put off his trip to the spa to see it performed. As some of the ladies were turning up their noses, I hear that he told them his mind."[50] Nevertheless, the play was a failure—indeed, the Berlin police suppressed it in 1814—and it soon vanished from the German and Austrian repertories. Only the opera based on it—Lortzing's *Der Wildschütz*—survived.

[47] Mathes 1969, p. 298.
[48] Kotzebue 1821, pp. 12-14.
[49] For these and other testimonials, see Stock 1971, p. 78, and Mathes 1972, pp. 597-598.
[50] W. von Kotzebue 1881, p. 71.

Die Prinzessin von Cacambo, written and published at about the same time as *Der Rehbock*, must have shocked the same people who were appalled by the latter. A couple of samples will suffice. The Mogul Prince and his harlequin Hurlibuck, both disguised as girls, are gaining access to the Princess, the sight of whom drives all men mad, by bribing her old nurse, Pulma.

PULMA. Now you wait here until the Princess comes out from her bath in order to take a little walk.
HURLIBUCK. Couldn't we attend her at her bath directly as a couple of honorable ladies?
PRINCE. That's right, my good woman, if it were possible—(II, 2)

And so on. A bit later, an old gardener suggests two preservatives against going out of one's mind: either get thoroughly drunk, or else —

HURLIBUCK. Well, let's hear it.
GARDENER. We have in our seraglio a pack of attendants with the prettiest clear voices. If you'll make up your minds to—
HURLIBUCK. No, no forget it. We'd rather just venture our *heads*. (II, 3)

This sort of jesting had been coin of the realm when that great *commedia* writer Nolan de Fatouville (even more thoroughly forgotten than Kotzebue) was creating scenarios for the Italian comedians who performed in Paris at the end of the seventeenth century; but in the German world, Victorian before Victoria, it had become unpresentable.

There is, I feel, a tragic link between Kotzebue's erotics and his politics. For in his political pamphlets his tone of voice is also, to a degree, that of a rococo madcap blindly wandering into a new universe dominated by the grimly serious voice of the Revolution. And it was perhaps this light, this frivolous style which turned out to be unbearable to the young and ardent liberals of the time. Was this what Goethe meant when, eleven years after Kotzebue's assassination, he said to Eckermann, "Kotzebue was for a long time an object of hatred, but for the student's dagger to be raised against him, certain journals must first have made him contemptible."[51]

An exotic testimony to Kotzebue's fame in these years is provided by Adelbert von Chamisso, who sailed round the world as a scientific observer with the playwright's son, Otto, from 1815 to 1818. His classic diary, published two years after Kotzebue's death, tells of American newspapers commenting on *The Stranger*—still!; of libraries in the Aleutians (private ones, I assume) that consist of nothing but a single volume by Kotzebue; of the governor of Manila

---

[51] *Conversations with Eckermann*, 15 February 1831.

entrusting Otto with a gift of the costliest coffee for his father in honor of the Muses; and of a sailor at Cape Horn announcing the arrival of a ship commanded by a captain bearing "a comedian's name."[52]

From Weimar Kotzebue now began to send his reports to Russia. The "literary commissar," as he has been called, was not performing any undercover work, but innocuously apprising the Tsar of what was being read and discussed in the West—the same task the Baron de Grimm had undertaken in the eighteenth century for Catherine II without being mistaken then or since for a spy. Presently, however, Kotzebue began to issue the last of his periodicals, the *Literarisches Wochenblatt* (Literary Weekly), in which he unremittingly and all too amusingly attacked the liberal tendencies of the day. Having battled many a literary enemy, and taken on Napoleon himself, without suffering bodily harm, Kotzebue could not sense that this time he was imperiling his life. Nor, in those days, was political assassination the commonplace event it is in our own times. Hostile students broke his windows in Weimar, to be sure, but he could not have imagined the "final solution." Besides, if the thought of political murder had crossed his mind, he would surely have reasoned, as did many observers afterwards, that there were far more important targets in Germany than a mere playwright.

But this was not apparent to young Karl Ludwig Sand, the idealistic student who had never read Kotzebue's plays and knew him only as a traitor in the Tsar's pay, the author of a reactionary *History of the German Reich* and of those vicious articles in the *Wochenblatt*—knew him, in his own words, as a "seducer of youth," an accusation drolly and sadly reminiscent of the public judgment against Socrates.

The final defeat of Napoleon had aroused strong hopes in Germany for far-reaching political, social, and economic reforms. The ideas were largely French in origin, and were freely called Jacobin by the conservatives, and yet those who espoused them had contributed enthusiastically to the war of liberation against the French emperor. The frightened rulers of Europe made liberal promises while they still needed the people; but once Napoleon had been exiled to Saint Helena, only Karl August gave his subjects in Weimar a genuine constitution and considerable freedom of speech. Since the University of Jena stood in his little duchy, it readily became a focus of agitation for all of Germany. Bitterly disappointed in their hopes, an elite of professors and students agitated, some tamely, some wildly, for constitutional government, taxation by consent of the Estates, abolition of aristocratic privileges, freedom of thought, speech and press, and even the unification of Germany.

Already during the French occupation, the schoolteacher and nationalist F. L. Jahn had organized the young in groups dedicated to the apparently harmless

---

[52] C. Von Kotzebue 1911, p. 101.

business of group gymnastics, which in actuality half-concealed a militant patriotic impulse. This youth movement contributed volunteers against the French, and after the wars became increasingly politicized. Several periodicals spread the liberal ideas. In 1815 the first *Burschenschaft*—we might translate the term as Youth Group—was created at Jena to study, discuss, and propagate nationalistic ideals. Similar organizations sprang up throughout Germany and kept in touch with one another. Most of these groups and their leaders remained distinctly non-revolutionary, and Marxist writers have strongly blamed them for their failure to organize the masses. Nevertheless, extremist subgroups inevitably appeared. Their members were called *Die Unbedingten*, that is to say, the Unconditionals or Implacables. Unlike their moderate brothers, who were modestly asking rulers and aristocrats to make concessions of their own free will, the extremists preached violence. Pamphlets and songs incited self-sacrificing patriots to murder noblemen:

> Freiheitmesser gezückt!
> Hurra! Den Dolch durch die Kehle gedrückt!

(Twitch, freedom's knife! Hurrah! The dagger pushed through the throat!)[53] In short, three movements, from least to most radical, were spreading throughout the land: the Athletic Associations (to use a modern term), the Youth Groups, and the cells of the Implacables.

The contemporary liberal—my probable reader, I venture to say—is likely to sympathize with this liberal movement after making a mental exception of the extremists. But the later history of Germany may cloud an easy verdict. Hostile observers were even then disturbed by the "Teutomania" of these groups. Strongly marked by the Romantic worship of the past, the young patriots exulted in a vision of a pure Protestant Germany guided by Luther's Bible. They dressed in ancient national costumes, tried to purge the language of ungermanic elements, disliked foreigners, Catholics, and Jews, and proclaimed the superiority of the German soul. We are likely to sympathize with their hatred of absolute rulers and their demand for a constitution, but what are we to say of their ferocious nationalism, their fanatical rallies, and their book-burning? Nothing is more naive than to make up a moral ledger for this period in German history marked Good and Evil, with "liberalism" under the first heading and "reaction" the convenient hate-word under the other. Out of the movement that rid the world of the reactionary Kotzebue and his easy-going, amused cosmopolitanism were to come the dreadful "theories" of Adolf Hitler at the low end of the intellectual spectrum and "that idiot Heidegger," as the vice-rector at Freiburg University called him, at the high end.

[53] Schröder 1967, p. 254.

The book-burning in question, anticipating the famous Nazi orgy of 1933, occurred at the climax of a remarkable occasion known as the Wartburg Celebration. In October 1817, costumed in old German garb, some four hundred students assembled at Eisenach where the grand fortress known as the Wartburg stands. They were celebrating the Allied victory over Napoleon at the Battle of Leipzig, to which Jahn's volunteers had contributed, and the tercentenary of Luther's 95 theses. It was at the Wartburg, too, that Luther had begun his translation of the Bible. There were gymnastic displays, festive meals, divine services, speeches, processions, and then a grand burning of infamous books. And there was jubilation as each book was taken from a basket and tossed into the fire after naming of author and title, and a brief commentary. One of the books was Kotzebue's *History of the German Reich*. Its author was described as a lackey of feudal absolutism. This was duly taken in by Sand, a veteran of "study groups" and patriotic meetings, who was seen carrying one of the banners onto the stage of the Knights Hall.

Every detail of the Wartburgfest had been reported to and by the press, and Kotzebue, though probably proud of the distinction his scholarly compilation had earned, had one more motive for needling in his weekly the youth movement in particular and liberal ideas in general. I give a sample here because it may remind us that history does, to some extent, repeat itself.

We admit that we cannot persuade ourselves that this so-called academic freedom is to be called noble and liberal. For in what does it consist? In nothing else than in the complete freedom for every student to live or not to live like a sloven, to attend or not attend classes, hence to learn something or not, to save his money or squander it, to pay his debts or defraud the townspeople, to dress decently or like a clown, all as he sees fit. What is noble about all this? And why do we send our sons to universities? Isn't it so they will do something solid? Such is the goal, the only goal, but nothing is done to achieve it except to have the Herr Professor get up and read, not worrying in the least whether anyone is listening to him, and indeed without the right to worry about it. . . . Truly, every father must tremble nowadays if the young man is lively and quick-witted, for lying in wait for him on all sides are the *Landsmannschaften* and *Burschenschaften*, the *Turnkunst*[54] and even the lecture-rooms, where injudicious professors tell him that he is called upon to reform his fatherland—and no one appears to reassure the anxious father concerning the use his son is making of his

---

[54] The *Landsmannschaften* were ancient student groups based on the boys' regional provenances. The new *Burschenschaften* effaced this particularism in favor of common national goals. *Bursch* simply means "lad." *Turnkunst* is, literally, the art of gymnastics, but Kotzebue is referring once more to the groups which exercised and trained together. As I have mentioned before, under French occupation these outwardly harmless athletics concealed a military and nationalistic subintention.

precious time. . . .

Nothing is more ridiculous and foolish than the contention that through the abolition of academic freedom (we call it license) human genius will lose the playground it needs for full development. . . . Genius breaks everywhere out of its bud. . . . Truly, every father who worries over his growing sons would give heartfelt thanks to the government that would make a beginning of banning students' self-determination from its universities. . . . Childless citizens too, who love peace and order would join their thankfulness to that of fathers . . . for— God preserve us in Germany from any revolution![55]

The incorrigible author of *Bahrdt* and *The Hyperborean Ass* was enjoying himself again. And nothing might have happened to him, had not his enemies got hold of one of his reports to Russia, published it in the review fatefully called *Nemesis*, and pinned the label of Russian spy on Kotzebue so vigorously that as late as in the 1894 edition of the Brockhaus encyclopaedia, the German public could still read that the Russians had sent him to Germany as a "police-political spy."[56]

Weimar and Jena now became too "hot" for him. After taking the baths at Pyrmont and visiting his estate in Estonia for the last time, the much-travelled Kotzebue settled in Mannheim toward the end of 1818. To this city then came the young terrorist, dressed in a traditional German jacket, carrying a page from the New Testament along with inflamed writings of his own, and armed with two long daggers. On March 23, 1819, he gained admittance to Kotzebue's study, where, as if enacting the song from which I have given two lines, he stabbed and slashed his victim to death with one of the knives, then, dashing into the street below, knelt and shouted, "Almighty God, I thank thee for allowing me to carry out this act of justice! Long live my German fatherland!" and stabbed himself with the other. He recovered in the hospital, however, and the authorities were obliged to create a martyr by beheading him.

Like a figure in one of his own melodramas, Kotzebue died as wife, children, and servants came rushing into the room where he lay in his blood. The murder was an unprecedented sensation. Goethe gave it four exclamation marks in his diary. But very little sympathy was expended on the dead reactionary, while Sand became a national hero. Indeed, the Mannheim executioner refused to touch him, and his colleague in nearby Heidelberg took the job only after Sand

[55] W. von Kotzebue 1881, pp. 113-114.

[56] Brückner 1975, p. 35. I find he is still called "a Russian informer" (not an informant!) in a *History of Prussia* by H. W. Koch published in 1978, a spy in the 1985 edition of the Columbia *History of the World*, and "the Tsar's secret agent" by Feilchenfeldt in his edition of Varnhagen von Ense's memoirs (Varnhagen 1987, III, 780). Varnhagen's circumstantial account of the crime and its aftermath, though tainted by his hatred of Kotzebue, is particularly useful because he was in Mannheim at the time as Prussian envoy to the court of Baden, and kept in close touch with the case from the very day of the murder. See Varnhagen 1987, III, pp. 411-450.

himself guaranteed his safety from the wrath of the students. To this day the killer is honored in a museum in his native town of Wunsiedel near Bayreuth, and in 1971 German television viewers were treated to Tankred Dorst's *Sand*, glorifying him all over.[57] Even those who objected to downright murder gave lofty explanations which redounded more to Sand's than to Kotzebue's benefit. Not untypically, Friedrich de la Motte Fouqué (1777-1843) issued a pamphlet condemning Sand because Kotzebue had been the wrong target. Goethe, never at a loss for oracular statements, spoke of "the superior world order,"[58] while thousands of letters went off to console the fanatic's mother. Few attended the "Todtenfeir" or Memorial Celebration arranged by the king at the Berliner Theater, at which Kotzebue's patriotic, anti-Napoleonic but strictly monarchical *Hermann und Thusnelda* (written in 1813) was performed as a benefit for the widow and children, yielding a modest one thousand taler—about a year's salary for a respectably placed official.[59] Thereafter, unfriendly history drops its impenetrable veil over mother and wife. The students, by the way, staged a Todtenfeir of their own for Sand in an open space in Berlin. In the Kurpfälzisches Museum of Heidelberg, which preserves Kotzebue's death mask, I have stood contemplating with a certain melancholy a series of colored prints depicting Sand's anointed journey to Mannheim, the murder, the hero in prison, and the decapitation. Many such prints were sold, pamphlets of all sorts appeared, and before long, the first *Life of Kotzebue*, written by a certain F. Cramer (1820) confirmed the playwright as the villain of the story.

The authorities, on the other hand, were thoroughly aroused. Seizing the convenient pretext, the German rulers formulated their notorious Carlsbad Decrees. Jahn and other leaders had already been arrested. Now the students groups were suppressed, the universities put under strict surveillance, and censorship was redoubled. The entire reform movement suffered a shock from which it did not recover for decades. This too posterity remembered against Kotzebue.

[57] Albertsen 1978, p. 223.
[58] Rabany 1893, p. 124.
[59] Geiger 1895, p. 399, where the play is erroneously called Kotzebue's last. According to Geiger, Kotzebue's family were "in a bad way" financially after the assassination. But it may be supposed that the trouble was temporary, since Kotzebue held ample possessions in the Baltic. In any event, the clan did not sink into obscurity: one of Kotzebue's sons, Otto (1787-1846), became the notable explorer who gave his name to an Alaskan gulf and town.

THE GOOD CITIZENS OF PIFFELHEIM

For the notes to *The Good Citizens of Piffelheim* I have availed myself selectively of annotations in the editions of *Die deutschen Kleinstädter* published by M. Bailly (1884), E. Lombard (1889), R. Guignard (1952), H. Schumacher (1954), and J. Mathes (1972). The first three of these are all I have seen of the seven German-language editions in twenty printings which appeared in France, where they were mainly used as schooltexts, between 1840 and 1952. The British Museum Catalogue lists two German-language editions printed in England—again with notes—one in 1857 and the other in 1884, but these I have also been unable to consult. On the other hand, I have made use of a considerable number of miscellaneous sources of information, most of which I have left unnamed in the interest of brevity.

Characters

Herr Nicholas Staar, Mayor, also Senior Church Elder of Piffelheim.
Frau Staar, his mother and the late Deputy Collector of the Revenue's widow.
Lotte, his daughter.
Herr Vice-Churchwarden Staar, his brother, a greengrocer.
Frau Brendel, the late Timber and Fishery Administrator's widow.
Frau Morgenroth, the late City Excise-Office Recorder's widow.
Herr Sperling, Assistant Inspector of Buildings, Roads, and Mines.
Karl Olmers.
A Night Watchman.
Klaus, the town bailiff.
Margaret, a maid.
A Farmhand.
Ursula and Gottlieb, the Mayor's small children.

The action occurs in the little town of Piffelheim in Prussia in the year 1801 or 1802. Acts One to Three take place in the Mayor's house; Act Four in the street before the house.

Note on Characters and Place

Lotte (diminutive Lottchen) was Sabine in the original, and Kotzebue's Margarete has lost her final 'e'. The other characters are unchanged. Staar and Sperling mean starling and sparrow, respectively, just as the Kräh- in Krähwinkel means crow. These uses of "illustrative" names (familiar to us from English comedy) are vestigial in the sense that, mercifully, Kotzebue does not pump them for humor. Hence little is lost by not translating them into English.

For the honorific titles, I have followed Kotzebue as closely as possible, without always succeeding in duplicating them. He would have been the last to worry about this difficulty. Klaus has been promoted from *Ratsdiener* ("town-council servant," that is to say, their Man Friday) to Bailiff, inasmuch as he is also the turnkey in charge of the cattle-thief.

As far as Krähwinkel is concerned, the original means Crow-Corner, and this I suppose is what induced Kotzebue to name two of his characters after birds. In German, as I have noted before, the name referred to a hick town long before Kotzebue used it, but he appears to have obtained it from a story by Jean Paul, published in 1801, in which a Krehwinkel is described as a pretty but very muddy, stony little provincial town. I have dropped the name for the simple reason that it means nothing to the unspecialized American or British reader.

No document is extant to point to any particular small town Kotzebue might have had in mind when the notion came to him to turn Picard's *La petite ville* to his own account, and none of his commentators have discussed the matter. To me, at any rate, a number of allusions suggest a location in the Prussian province of Silesia: references to timber, mines, fisheries, textile works, hops and beets, and Hussite invasions. Furthermore, the distance from Berlin seems to be right. But Kotzebue might also have drawn in his imagination upon towns in Saxony (he complained more than once about the bad condition of its roads) or, for that matter, in Estonia.

ACT 1[1]

Lotte is standing alone at the window. Suddenly she slams it shut and runs to [1]
the door.

LOTTE. Margaret, Margaret!

MAID (*outside*). What is it, Miss?

LOTTE. The mail has arrived. Run and see if there are letters for me. (*To herself*) Five weeks have passed since I came home from Berlin[2] and I've not
had a single word from him. If I'm disappointed again today—I'll—I'll
what?—I'll lose my temper—and marry Sperling. Gently, gently! I can
lose my temper without marrying Sperling. Why should I be the one to be
punished?

MAID. Here's a letter for you, Miss Lotte. [2]

LOTTE (*tears the letter out of her hand*). At last! At last! (*She sees the
handwriting*) From my cousin!

MAID. I brought the newspapers too. (*She places them on the table*) Everybody and his brother seems to be writing letters—sixteen of them today,
says the Postmaster—each one of them addressed to Piffelheim. He's
going out of his mind!

LOTTE. That will do, Margaret.

(*Exit the maid*)

LOTTE (*Alone. She skims the letter*). "A new play." Who cares? "Dresses now [3]
have the longest trains." Who wants to know? "English straw hats." Who
asked her? What? That's all?—not a word about *him*? Granted, I for-
bade him to write directly to me—it didn't seem right—but he promised to
let my cousin . . . and she promised too . . . why didn't either one keep his
word? Am I forgotten already? He was going to appear in person with
letters of introduction from his Lordship—and now he has neither come
nor written. And yet he knows that I'm being married off to Sperling.
Father is tormenting me. Grandmother is tormenting me. And now
Olmers is tormenting me too. (*She crumples up the letter*) Serves you
right. You've been warned often enough to beware of these Berlin play-
boys. They fall in love three times a day, but by evening, on their way to
the playhouse, they've forgotten all about it. Oh Karl, Karl, are you just

---

[1] Kotzebue uses the continental mode of subdividing acts into scenes which are numbered according
to significant entrances or exits. I have retained these numbers in the margin for quick reference.

[2] Kotzebue never calls the city by its name, even though the presence of a king leaves no doubt that
we are in Prussia and that the *Residenz* (the seat of government) is Berlin. Why the vagueness? Because a few sallies are directed at the Court (see I, 9 and I, 14)? Or as normal procedure for the
"universalizing" neo-classical artist?

another young nobody? Good at flowery babble and nothing more? (*She draws a portrait from her pocket*) Can these features deceive? With this very look in his eyes he swore to come here in a few weeks and to win my father. Are five weeks "a few"? Must I do his arithmetic for him and show him that five weeks add up to thirty-five eternal days? Oh Karl, hurry. Otherwise you've lost me. (*She looks mournfully at the portrait*)

[4]   (*Enter Frau Staar*)

FRAU STAAR. Lottchen, the cakes are out of the oven. They're heavenly and will do you proud. Now we'll decorate them with flowers and sprinkle them with sprigs of myrtle.[3] I needn't tell you why. There will be such a feast tomorrow—a stupendous feast. But you're staring at me like a sick canary. Didn't you hear me? What's this in your hand?

LOTTE (*frightened, wants to hide the portrait*). Nothing, dear granny.

FRAU STAAR. Poppycock! I saw something like a spectacle case. Give it to me. At once! I *will* have it.

LOTTE (*giving it*). It's a portrait.

FRAU STAAR. A portrait of a man? God help me! Child—don't let me suppose—

LOTTE. Suppose what?

FRAU STAAR. I'll make an uproar in the house. I'll scream fire.

LOTTE. For God's sake, don't, dearest granny. (*Waggishly*) Suppose there *is* a fire. How will screaming put it out?

FRAU STAAR. A stranger's portrait in your pocket! And in your heart too, is he?

LOTTE. All it is is a man under glass in a frame.

FRAU STAAR. Don't tell me about men. They jump out of frames before you can count to one. So there we have it. I always did object to your being sent to Berlin. When I was a young girl—a well-educated young girl—all I knew about the capital was that His Majesty, the King, lives in it. A fine kettle of fish. The girl brings pictures home—pictures of men. You godless wench! Do you understand what this thing means? When I was your age nobody had his portrait painted unless he had rank and position or had been married for at least ten years. And even then it was done with dignity. A life-size portrait, a lace ruff about the neck and a posy in his hand. That is how your grandfather hangs to this day behind the kitchen cupboard—as Deputy Collector of the Revenue, may he rest in peace. But nowadays, God help us! these youngsters are having their picture done with dishevelled hair and shirts wide open. And they do it in miniature— so small you can hide them in a needle box. That is where the mischief begins. Life-size portraits stand decently in the open for all the world to

---

[3] In anticipation of the myrtle leaves Lotte will wear in her hair on her wedding day, like all German brides since time immemorial.

see. But these miniature devils sneak into everybody's pockets and even, God forgive me, hang from ribbons and chains on people's bosoms. Who is he? Out with it!

LOTTE (*embarrassed*). Grandmother dear, you're anxious about nothing at all—

FRAU STAAR. Out with it. Who is he?

LOTTE. It's—(*aside*) What shall I tell her? (*Aloud*) It's a picture of our King.

FRAU STAAR. Our King?

LOTTE. Cousin Emily sent it to me because she knows how we all love him.

FRAU STAAR. Oh! Well now! That's something else. So this—this is our King. I've always longed to feast my eyes on him. But how is it he's not wearing the star around his neck?

LOTTE. He feels he can shine without it.

FRAU STAAR. Well, that was very clever of your cousin. Lottchen, dear, I want you to make me a present of the picture. I'll take it out of its frame and pin it to my cap.

LOTTE (*aside*). What shall I do?

FRAU STAAR. I'll lend it to you on your wedding day—or even tomorrow for your engagement. (*She pockets the picture*)

LOTTE. No, thank you. I'd rather never wear it at all. Only spare me the engagement.

FRAU STAAR. Right you are, Lottchen. Be coy. Drop a tear. Hide in a corner. That's how a young lady should behave. That's how *I* behaved. Nowadays young girls stare straight into their sweethearts' eyes and talk about engagements as if they were giving out a recipe for almond tarts. One's lucky if they do a little fainting in church on their wedding day.

LOTTE. But I'm not playing coy, grandmother. I can't stand Herr Sperling. He sticks to me like a burr. He chatters like a magpie—in short, he's an idiot.

FRAU STAAR. Hush up and mind your tongue. I've known more than one sharp-tongued hussy who lived to thank her stars when the butt of her jokes led her up to the altar.

LOTTE. I'd rather remain single.

FRAU STAAR. Good grief! What objections can you raise against the man? Doesn't he have a lovely title? Isn't he Assistant Inspector of Buildings, Roads, and Mines?

LOTTE. I don't care.

FRAU STAAR. Weren't his parents respectable people? His grandfather sat in the town council.

LOTTE. Good for him.

FRAU STAAR. You'll come into a heap of new relatives.

LOTTE. So much the worse.

FRAU STAAR. Cousins, uncles, aunts—one helpful with this, the other helpful with that. . . .

LOTTE. A family dinner once a week.

FRAU STAAR. Which is also nice. And you'll give your own, second to none. You'll have sumptuous table linen for eighteen guests. And Herr Sperling's good silver pieces. He's no pauper, you know. He owns a vegetable garden outside the town gate and a family plot in the churchyard.

LOTTE. I wish he were lying in it this moment.

FRAU STAAR. You God-forsaken girl! Here comes your uncle. He'll tell you what a sweet little man is our Assistant to the Inspector of Buildings, Roads, and Mines.

[5]   (*Enter Vice-Churchwarden Staar*).

FRAU STAAR. Good morning, Andreas my son. Come here. Since you're our Vice-Churchwarden and know how to string words together, you're the man to enlighten this silly goose. She wants nothing to do with her engagement and makes jokes at the bridegroom's expense.

HERR STAAR. What's this I hear?

LOTTE. Uncle Andreas will side with me. As the owner of a circulating library, he knows the ways of the world.

HERR STAAR. Indeed I do.

LOTTE. And, having read all the new novels, he sees into the human heart.

HERR STAAR. I do indeed.

LOTTE. He will tell you right off how many a poor girl who was forced to marry against her will died of consumption.

HERR STAAR. No, my dear, this is not the kind of novel I keep in my circulating library. Sentimental novels are *out*. I'm using them to wrap groceries in my shop. Crime is what people want—bloody murderers.

FRAU STAAR. God preserve us.

HERR STAAR. The only trouble is that our writers aren't as patriotic as they should be. They're always glorifying wicked Italians as if we didn't have our own thieves and highwaymen — great Germans all.[4]

FRAU STAAR. To be sure, ten years ago there was Lorenz Schmeckebein who was hanged right here from our own gallows.

HERR STAAR. Exactly, mother. Between you and me, I've been turning him into a play. Sperling is writing the lyrics. He's quite a poet, Sperling is. Especially with sonnets. He makes those words rhyme even if he has to kick them.

FRAU STAAR. Did you hear that, Lotte?

[4] Wicked Italians populated the horror and mystery fiction in Germany just as they did in England. Herr Staar proposes two notorious German bandits instead: Christian Andreas Käsebier, whom Frederick the Great of Prussia employed but whom the Austrians executed in 1757, and Johannes Bückler, known as Schinderhannes ("the knacker"), head of a gang of plunderers in the Rhineland and still alive at the time *Die deutschen Kleinstädter* was written: he was executed in 1803. Lorenz Schmeckebein (suggesting "tasty leg") is Kotzebue's invention.

HERR STAAR. A good little fellow, our Sperling; knows all about the latest literature waves, he could lecture at the University.

FRAU STAAR. Did you hear that?

HERR STAAR. He's a fountain of iambics, a cascade of pentameters[5] —I'd like to see anybody turning them out quicker than he does.

FRAU STAAR. What *now*, Lottchen, eh?

HERR STAAR. To sum up, my girl, he's going to be your husband, my nephew, my heir, and my helper in the circulating library— period.

(Enter the Mayor) [6]

MAYOR. Lotte, fetch me my wig. I'm on my way to City Hall.

LOTTE. Right away, my dear papa. *(Exits)*

MAYOR. How do you do, brother Andreas.[6] What a rotten day! They're making me work like a farm-horse.

HERR STAAR. Is that right?

MAYOR. Everything rests on my shoulders—the entire city's well-being. Today I'm deciding the case between Barsch and the night watchman, the one about the broken lantern.

HERR STAAR. In whose favor are you deciding?

MAYOR. The night watchman has to repair the lantern and Barsch has to pay the court costs, four taler and eight groschen.[7]

FRAU STAAR. Very fair.

MAYOR. After that I have to deal with Korb, the shoemaker, and Lummel, the tailor, because of the fist-fight in the tavern.

HERR STAAR. And your decision?

MAYOR. Both keep the blows they got and both pay the fine.

FRAU STAAR. Very just.

MAYOR. Then comes that business where it's me against everybody.

HERR STAAR. You mean the street cleaning affair.

---

[5] Herr Staar's description of Sperling's talents is freely adapted here from a series of key words and phrases which "in" spectators and readers of the time would immediately have pinned on the Schlegel brothers: *Sonnetten, Romanzen, Fragmente,* and *die neuere Aesthetik* (the New Aesthetic). These are among the passages Goethe would not admit on the Weimar stage. Today most Germans need footnotes for them like everyone else. But Kotzebue must have been perfectly aware that the dialogue survives on stage even if one does not catch the specific allusions.

[6] Literally, "I am your servant, sir brother." Throughout the play, the Staars and their relations will be addressing each other with a solemn (and, in context, comical) formality which idiomatic English can only approximate, even if we draw on the language spoken by the characters, say, of Jane Austen's novels. What is at stake is nothing less than a social contract: my formality towards you gives you status, yours towards me gives it to me.

[7] There were 24 groschen in the taler. I can find no way of conveying this bit of humor in the unmediated text. A copy of *Die deutschen Kleinstädter* fetched 16 groschen, and for two taler one could purchase a typical small volume of Kotzebue's plays or two pair of very plain shoes. In short, the four taler eight groschen are a trifling amount of money for the bourgeoisie; and yet, they cover about two weeks' salary for a Berlin journeyman. For more on monetary values, see notes 10 and 18.

MAYOR. Precisely. Our honorable town council flatly refuses to involve itself
in street cleaning. It seems it's been each individual's task since the beginning of the world to clean his own muck and the honorable municipal
council will lie in said muck without budging until the troublemakers do
their duty.

FRAU STAAR. Let each one sweep his own doorstep; it's an old saying.

MAYOR. No, my dear mama, I'm the Mayor, also Senior Church Elder, and I
do *not* sweep my own doorstep. Let them appeal—the muck stays where it
is. I don't care if the action takes twenty years to settle, my muck won't
move an inch.

HERR STAAR. A man must stick to what's right.

MAYOR. Well spoken, brother.

FRAU STAAR. But in the end we won't be able to open the front door
anymore.

MAYOR. That suits me perfectly. We'll stay home. Then let them see how
they'll manage at City Hall. I'm as firm as the Great Wall of China.[8] What
would have happened to our privileges long ago if it hadn't been for me?
Who brought matters to the point where tomorrow the whole town is toast-
ing its victory? *I* did. That's who. It's *I* who rammed it through. It's *I* who
saved Piffelheim's honor.

[7]   (*Enter Lotte with the wig*)

LOTTE. Here's your wig.

FRAU STAAR. You haven't changed your mind, son, have you, about celebrating Lotte's betrothal at the same time?

MAYOR. I certainly haven't. It's going to be a memorable day.

FRAU STAAR. Miss, here, is raising objections.

MAYOR. How's that? I'm the Mayor, also Senior Church Elder. Nobody
raises objections to my face.

LOTTE. Dear papa!

MAYOR. Duty before Love. I belong to the State. It devolves on me to bring
lustre to a celebration that's going to shower blessings down to our great-
grandchildren. (*As he puts on his wig*) This question of jurisdiction
between our beloved Piffelheim and the magistrates of our neighbors in
Rummelsburg was hotly contested— a female thief had been arrested—we
wanted to stick her in the pillory, so did the Rummelsburger—we wanted
to whip her, so did the Rummelsburger—nine years we've been at law
with them—the delinquent party has been kept safe under lock and key all
these years—thank God she's still alive—we triumphed at last, and tomorrow she'll sit in *our* pillory.

LOTTE. Dear father, your delinquent party can't feel worse than I do.

---

[8] Kotzebue has the Babylonian Wall, a structure erected six centuries before Christ.

MAYOR. How so?

LOTTE. After she's endured her punishment, she's free. I, on the other hand, haven't committed any crime. Yet tomorrow I am to be loaded down with chains to my dying day.

MAYOR. Calm yourself, my dear. The pagan god Amor or Hymenaeus forges none but flower-chains.

LOTTE. Which not infrequently oppress the heart.

MAYOR. Herr Assistant Inspector of Buildings, Roads, and Mines Sperling is a man of value to the city.

FRAU STAAR. That's what I keep saying.

MAYOR. He is not wanting in *judicio*.[9]

HERR STAAR. That's what I keep saying.

MAYOR. He is a man of property.

FRAU STAAR. My words exactly!

MAYOR. Produces all manner of *exercitia* in verse.

FRAU STAAR. Spoken after my own heart.

MAYOR. To conclude: I have chosen the aforementioned as my son-in-law and no further dilatory objections are to be adduced.

LOTTE (*aside*). Oh God, everything is in league against me.

(*Enter the maid*)   [8]

MAID. One of the farmhands is at the door with a letter. The man who sent it is lying in the quarry raising the devil. His carriage is smashed up and so's one of his legs, I think.

MAYOR. Ever since I've been Mayor, also Senior Church Elder, not a week has gone by—praise the Lord—without some traveler overturned on our highway.

FRAU STAAR. Why doesn't the town council have it repaired?

MAYOR. And what would become of our blacksmiths and saddlers whose bread and butter depends on overturned travelers?

LOTTE. But the travelers keep complaining, father dear, and to make matters worse, they're obliged to pay toll.

MAYOR. Let them complain and pay. What right have they to talk when *we* have to put up with our Piffelheim streets, and they twice as broken down as the highway?

LOTTE. In spite of the pavement tax.

MAYOR. There you have it. We too fracture our bones and yet we don't

---

[9] The Mayor will be using a bit of Latin as often as he can think of any. Kotzebue must have remembered his own legal training at Jena in 1779-1780, and the disputations which were a part of that training. "These learned tussles were in the Latin tongue," he wrote much later. "It was kitchen Latin to be sure, but we learned to babble in Latin, and in particular we became familiar with legal expressions." Thanks to these scraps, he adds, he was able to pass the bar (as we would say today). See Kotzebue 1922, p. 177, and note 14 for Act Four. I give the Mayor's Latin only where this presents no problem to the lay audience today.

grumble. All right, where's that letter?

[9] (*Enter a farmhand*)

FARMHAND. Begging forgiveness of Your Worship, a fellow is sprawled down in the quarry. I'm guessing it's somebody respectable because there's lanterns on his coach and they're broken too.

MAYOR. What about the arms and legs?

FARMHAND. They seem to be all right for once. Only the nose is a wee bit damaged.

MAYOR. And the carriage?

FARMHAND. Looks awful. One wheel ran all the way to the sign where turnpike tolls are posted.

HERR STAAR. He can read them to while his time away.

FARMHAND. Oh, as for reading, he's got heaps of books—all mucked up like his clothes. That's why he hasn't dared show himself yet to Your Worship.

MAYOR. What does he want of me?

FARMHAND. He gave me half a guilder[10] to announce him.

FRAU STAAR. He may have come to attend tomorrow's celebration.

LOTTE (*aside*). Or else perhaps—oh, my heart is pounding.

MAYOR (*opening the letter*). What's this—from His Excellency, the Prime Minister,[11] our patron and mainstay? Be silent, marvel, and attend. (*Reading*) "My dear Mayor." Yes, His Excellency has always held me dear. "The gentleman who will present this letter to you, my old high school and university friend, Herr Olmers—"

LOTTE (*aside*). Olmers at last![12]

FRAU STAAR. Plain Herr Olmers, a friend of His Excellency?

MAYOR. Silence. (*Reads*) "Has heard high praise of yourself and your municipality and wishes to spend a few weeks in it." Did you hear that, children? In Berlin they talk about nothing but our home town. "Inasmuch as I love and esteem Herr Olmers, I am asking you, as a particular favor"—

---

[10] I have Englished the word *Gulden*. Half a guilder was equal to 8 groschen or a third of a taler. The idea conveyed to the audience is that Olmers has tipped generously: enough for the messenger to buy a couple of very decent meals at his favorite tavern in Piffelheim. See notes 7 and 18.

[11] Kotzebue uses the expression "The directing [or chief] Herr Minister." In II, 6 this personage will be called the *Premierminister*, i.e., Prime Minister. As far as I know, such a post did not exist in Prussia at that time. A General Directorate of ministers governed the land, nominally under the King's Cabinet. But the term Prime Minister was applied if and when a particularly strong personality dominated the Directorate. All these officials were noblemen, while a man like Olmers would rise in the ranks as a commoner councillor, though he could hope to be ennobled (like Goethe and like Kotzebue) in the course of his career.

[12] As far as bare plot-structure is concerned, the accident in the quarry is a superfluity; Olmers might have presented himself without it, unscathed. But of such superfluities—witness Molière—good comedies are often made. This one came to Kotzebue from Picard, and, as a sort of alley leading to the main structure, it was clearly too good to suppress. Besides, it gave Kotzebue a chance to introduce his important secondary theme, that of civic corruption and maladministration.

your humble servant—"to lodge him in your own house"—Your Excellency has but to command—"to satisfy such needs as he may express to the best of your abilities"—will be done—

LOTTE (*aside*). Thank heaven!

MAYOR (*reading*). —"and to consider him as your own son." So be it. "It shall be my pleasure to seize upon any opportunity that comes my way to repay you this favor"—too kind—"In the meantime, my worthy Herr Mayor, I remain deeply obliged to you. Count von Hochberg." All this *manu propria*—in his own handwriting. Were you listening? His Excellency, Count von Hochberg—

FRAU STAAR. "Deeply obliged!"

HERR STAAR. "Worthy Herr Mayor!"

MAYOR. "To seize upon any opportunity!" *There* is a man for you, my children. *There* is a man fit to be mayor of Piffelheim any day. But he'll find out that I'm somebody too. (*To the farmhand*) Forward march! On your way! Convey my most humble respects to the stranger and tell him I am placing my coach at his disposal immediately.

FRAU STAAR. What are you thinking of? Our horses are in the field loading potatoes.

MAYOR. Right! Damn it. Run, instead, to the landlord of the Golden Cat. Have him harness fresh horses, put on his uniform of the Piffelheim Marksmen,[13] take the reins in his own hands, ride out, pick up, and bring back. Away! Away!

(*Exit farmhand*)

LOTTE (*aside*). He did keep his word.

FRAU STAAR. Son, the only point I object to is that you sent the stranger your most humble respects. Too much is too much.

MAYOR. Too much? Isn't the man a friend of the Count? And doesn't the Count wish to seize upon any opportunity to repay?

FRAU STAAR. All well and good. But the man is a nobody. Untitled, without position, plain Herr Olmers, while you are the Mayor, also Senior Church Elder.

MAYOR. You're right. But what's to be done? The farmhand has run off with my most humble respects.

HERR STAAR. Mother, in my opinion, there's more to this than meets the eye. If this Herr Olmers were nothing better than plain Herr Olmers, His Excellency would be damned before he'd worry about his welfare. High school and university friend indeed! God in heaven, these well-bred gentlemen

---

[13] So I translate the *Schützengilde* uniform Kotzebue mentions. I follow Lombard and Guignard in supposing that the innkeeper belongs to a club of marksmen. (Bailly, at a loss, speaks of a fire brigade!). In I, 13 they are said to have dances, presumably in their own hall. They clearly use the target-practice range mentioned in II, 2, and their banner is spoken of in II, 5.

don't even remember the folk they met the day before. So it says in all the
novels. Can you see them minding people they construed Latin with twenty
years ago?[14] No, sir. I'm convinced that Herr Olmers is traveling incognito and is a man of consequence in Berlin.

MAYOR. Good thinking, brother! Just watch. This stranger is at least a
member of the Cabinet.

HERR STAAR. Before you know it, he opens his coat—and out pops his Grand
Cross.

FRAU STAAR. His Grand Cross? I'm going to have one of my dizzy spells.

LOTTE (*aside*). It's a fact that he wears something precious on that spot.

FRAU STAAR. But tell me. What can he be looking for in Piffelheim?

MAYOR. Why? Are we short on cultural attractions? A townhall built in 1430
in which a general of the Hussites[15] once slapped the Mayor's face—

HERR STAAR. And the whalebone hanging from the ceiling—

MAYOR. And the town clock on which the cock crows and Saint Peter nods
his head—

FRAU STAAR. And our bleaching grounds—

HERR STAAR. And the prize antlers of that stag—

MAYOR. Shot by a Duke of Pomerania with his own noble hand.

FRAU STAAR. He might also be coming for the fabrics we produce in Piffelheim, don't you think?

MAYOR. Fiddle-faddle! A gentleman of his kind has seen fabrics enough in his
life.

FRAU STAAR. Well, he's sure to marvel at the cup of chicory I'll serve him.

HERR STAAR. While he reads a book out of my lending library—

MAYOR. Or the minutes of our sessions, where we handle some of the prickli-
est concerns of any town council in the land.

FRAU STAAR. Can you imagine the noise this will make in town—to have
such a man take up residence with us?

MAYOR. We'll have to entertain him in a manner befitting his rank.

HERR STAAR. Lottchen, have the children dressed in white. I'll send Sperling
over to teach them how to spread blossoms—it's the fashion nowadays.

MAYOR. While I alert the watchman and tell him to blow his bugle from the
tower. I'll have him blow his lungs out the moment the stranger crosses
the town gate.

[14] Kotzebue specifies Cornelius Nepos, the Roman historian.

[15] The followers of Jan Huss, the Bohemian reformer, turned to violence after the execution of their
leader in 1415. In 1426 and 1427 their general, Prokop the Great, defeated the German armies near
Silesia and began a series of incursions into Silesia and Saxony. Both Saxony and Silesia were invaded in 1430. Kotzebue was evidently making himself familiar with this material, for soon after
writing *Die deutschen Kleinstädter* he began work on his melodrama *The Hussites before Naumburg.*
Saxon Naumburg will appear a bit later in this scene in connection with its vineyards. As I mentioned before, it may well be that Piffelheim partakes of both Saxony and Silesia.

HERR STAAR. If I can find Sperling, I'll make him turn out a poem for the occasion.

MAYOR. Look for him, brother. As for you, mother, and you, daughter, betake yourselves to the kitchen and boil, broil, bake, and roast away. Lock up the pewter and take out the china. Place all the silver we own on the table. You can use my sterling snuff box as a salt-cellar. Set the tankard with my monogram before the stranger. A stack of rolls and no black bread. Two of my best bottles of Naumburger. A calf's head with a gilt laurel leaf in his snout. A mushroom pie and a roasted goose with crab apples. We'll prove to His Excellency that we know what's right and proper.

FRAU STAAR. And as far as urging him to partake is concerned, leave it to me. I'll urge as long as I can force another morsel down his throat. I'll urge until all his buttons pop.

MAYOR. Do so, mother. Brother, come with me. Let each one perform his appointed task and bring honor and renown to our beloved Piffelheim. (*Exit with Herr Staar*)

FRAU STAAR. Come alive, Lottchen. The damask table-cloth and napkins [10] have to go on the table. We *were* going to keep them until tomorrow especially for your engagement party—

LOTTE. Oh well. You never know what might happen today, granny dear.

FRAU STAAR. Is that so? Suddenly you're singing another tune. Because of the stranger, I suppose.

LOTTE. Of course, the stranger.

FRAU STAAR. Shall we invite him to the wedding?

LOTTE. That goes without saying.

FRAU STAAR. We'll place him at the head of the table.

LOTTE. No, he shall sit next to *me*.

FRAU STAAR. You can't do that, child. Next to you sits the bridegroom.

LOTTE. You're so right, dearest granny.

FRAU STAAR. And on the other side of you sits the bride's papa, *I* sit across the table from you, and he can sit next to me.

LOTTE. Well, I'll show him a little place he won't complain of.

FRAU STAAR. Who knows? He might do a good turn to your future husband.

LOTTE. I'm sure he will.

FRAU STAAR. There's been so much talk about Sperling becoming Assessor to the Beetroot Commission. What a lovely title that would be.

LOTTE. A very sweet title. Did you say the damask table-cloth?

FRAU STAAR. Yes, dear. I spun the thread for it myself at the time I was engaged to your grandfather. He used to sit beside me as I spun.

LOTTE. And sometimes the thread would snap?

FRAU STAAR. Wicked girl. Well, sometimes—

LOTTE. I'll get the damask and think about true love. (*Exit*)

[11] FRAU STAAR (*alone*). Well, well. Our Lottchen has suddenly come to life. But she's right. We have to bustle. Oh Lord! It just came to me—we must have some guests at the table—we can't possibly ask the stranger to dine all alone with us. But who should be invited? Everybody's gone. This is an important matter—whose advice shall I ask? Margaret! Margaret!

(*Enter the maid*)

FRAU STAAR. Run at once to Widow Timber and Fishery Administrator Brendel, then to Widow City Excise-Office Recorder Morgenroth and deliver the following message: Frau Deputy Collector of the Revenue Staar wishes to pay her respects to the Frau Timber and Fishery Administrator and the Frau City Excise-Office Recorder and if the Frau Timber and Fishery Administrator and the Frau City Excise-Office Recorder would have the kindness to call briefly on the Frau Deputy Collector of the Revenue, the Frau Deputy Collector of the Revenue would acknowledge their visit with heartfelt gratitude, inasmuch as an event of great importance has just occurred.

(*Exit the maid*)

FRAU STAAR (*alone*). Now I'll slip into my gala dress[16] with the little flowers that I wore when Nicholas was confirmed—a change of bonnets—but that wigmaker!—God have mercy—he won't come except on Sundays and holidays—during the week he runs about the countryside combing out all the pastors' wigs. What shall I do? I could ask Lotte to help—but the shocking fashion today—all those curls—a woman looks like a poodle— they won't plaster the hair down nice and neat, nor add pomade—nor part it in the middle—well, my son hasn't any thought in his head either. If he'd allowed the fine gentleman to flounder in his stone-pit for another couple of hours I could have received him with becoming gravity.

[12] (*Enter Frau Brendel*)

FRAU BRENDEL. Here I am, my dear, dear cousin[17] —after running all the way (emoh, I'm all out of breath. . . . I was drinking my cup of coffee— only my seventh this morning—yet I dropped everything—

FRAU STAAR. Much obliged, my dear. Did you know that—

---

[16] Frau Staar refers to a flowered *Kontusche*, an eighteenth-century gala dress. The word is Polish, and the dress was called a *polonaise* in France and England. In Scene 13, Frau Brendel is going to bespeak a roberonde, a similar formal dress dating back to the first half of the century. Frau Staar's wig is equally or almost equally outmoded and provincial. Wigs faded away around the time of the French Revolution, although clergymen and magistrates hung on to them. In England, indeed, they appear to have gone out of fashion—high fashion, that is—more than ten years earlier: see, for instance, the opening scene of Sheridan's *The Rivals* (1775). Nevertheless, Kotzebue saw wigs on men and women in Paris in 1804 (as a counter-revolutionary gesture under the First Consul, one wonders?), and our play itself, which can be relied upon, makes it clear that with respect to hairpieces, this was a transitional period.

[17] Everybody is vaguely everybody else's relative in Krähwinkel—within each separate social layer, of course.

FRAU BRENDEL. Yes. I know everything. My maid was doing her marketing when the butcher told her that his neighbor, the linen weaver, had overheard the townhall messenger telling his daughter: Nelly, he told her, two Counts are lying in the quarry with broken arms and legs and they'll be here within the hour. The watchman is going to blow his bugle, the children will be strewing flowers, the municipal authorities are leaving in a body to meet the Counts halfway and all the bells will be rung.

FRAU STAAR. One man, my dear. There is only one man out there in the quarry, presumably a gentleman, and he will be lodging with us. The Prime Minister himself has written a letter to my son, begging the favor in God's name. I'll let you guess at the turmoil in our house. And everything falls into my lap, everything!

(Enter Frau Morgenroth) [13]

FRAU MORGENROTH. Your servant, my best of cousins. I'm all flushed from running—I hope I haven't arrived too late. I was practically in my night shift—pardon my mentioning it—combing Fido and singing a morning hymn. At the third verse in rushes your maid. Goodness gracious, I thought the house was on fire. I jumped up, the dog fell off my lap, the hymnal dropped into the fire pan on which I was warming up my coffee, the coffee spilled into the coals, and two verses of "Awake My Heart and Sing" burned to a crisp.

FRAU STAAR. I'm infinitely sorry, my dear—

FRAU MORGENROTH. Please don't give it another thought. I know everything already. Three or four Princes are stretched out in the stone-pit. One of them is dead, another breathing his last, the coachman's neck is broken and the horses are done for. I have it all from Herr Balg, the solicitor whom I met in the street and who had it from his cook who had it from the Lottery-Inspector's wife, whose husband got all the details from his barber.

FRAU STAAR. Well, well, things are not as bad as all that. A farmer came here a while ago—

FRAU BRENDEL. I know. Imagine! He'd been given a full taler for a tip!

FRAU MORGENROTH. Five,[18] I assure you, cousin.

FRAU STAAR. He'd run as fast as he was able—

FRAU BRENDEL. So that he got a stitch in the side.

FRAU MORGENROTH. And a nose bleed.

FRAU STAAR. A gentleman had had a mishap with his carriage.

FRAU BRENDEL. A Count—

[18] A *louisd'or* in the original, corresponding to five taler. The actual tip, we remember, was half a guilder, equivalent to a third of a taler. We can infer, therefore, that Frau Brendel's report of a full taler would have been understood by the audience as a truly royal tip, and five times that as downright farcical. I have tried to convey something of these notions by adding "Imagine!" and "full" to the German. See notes 7 and 10.

FRAU MORGENROTH. Several Princes.

FRAU STAAR. That's more than we know so far. What is certain is that he is a man of quality, since he's not stopping at The Golden Cat but here—and this upon specific request from the highest quarters. Now: since my son, the Mayor, also Senior Church Elder, represents, so to speak, the Number One dignitary of Piffelheim, you can understand, my dear ladies, that he must bring luster to his rank.

FRAU BRENDEL. A banquet at City Hall—

FRAU MORGENROTH. The Marksmen ball—

FRAU STAAR. Tomorrow, as you know, is the grand celebration.

FRAU BRENDEL. Oh yes!—the woman who stole the cow nine years ago—

FRAU MORGENROTH. And who is being exposed in the pillory tomorrow. I'm simply thrilled.

FRAU BRENDEL. I had a brand new elegant dress[19] made for the occasion.

FRAU STAAR. All manner of preparations are on foot for these festivities. But today the honor of Piffelheim rests on our shoulders alone; today it's *our* duty to entertain, and entertain we shall with God's help. Let the tables sag under God's plenty. And you, my very special friends and neighbors, are invited.

FRAU BRENDEL. A tremendous honor—

FRAU MORGENROTH. You can count on me.

FRAU STAAR. My next wish is to acquaint the gentleman-stranger with our best people. And I am here to beg for your valued advice as to who should be invited.

FRAU BRENDEL. Let me see. You might ask—

FRAU MORGENROTH. I'd suggest—

FRAU BRENDEL. Herr Transport- and Land-Tax-Commissioner Kropf.

FRAU STAAR. Certainly not. Herr Kropf didn't think fit to invite us to the last dinner he gave his mother on her birthday.

FRAU BRENDEL. Oh my!

FRAU MORGENROTH. Why not Herr Wittmann, The Substitute Secretary to the Board of Management?

FRAU BRENDEL. I'm sorry, dear, but my late husband and Herr Wittmann's father-in-law litigated over a rain gutter.

FRAU MORGENROTH. Oh. Then we musn't.

FRAU STAAR. I was thinking of Herr Postal-Parcel-Examiner Holbein.

FRAU MORGENROTH. Don't invite *him* for God's sake! His wife is unbearable. A new dress almost every Sunday and swashing all over the pews—

FRAU BRENDEL. With her nose in the air—

FRAU MORGENROTH. Though one knows all about her—

---

[19] The *roberonde* mentioned in note 16. Only a footnote, alas, can catch the idea that it was an antiquated dress.

FRAU BRENDEL. Oh yes—when she was still in her farmgirl's apron[20] —

FRAU MORGENROTH. As for how she gets the wherewithal, well, one hears all kinds of rumors.

FRAU BRENDEL. I'd rather propose Herr Runkel, the Receiver of the Quarterly Acreage and Liquor Tax.

FRAU STAAR. Don't even mention the man, *please*—that boor! Do you think he so much as paid his respects to us? The puppy! He left his card one day. Nothing but his card. I'd rather invite the Timber-Float Fine-Collection Director Weidenbaum.

FRAU BRENDEL. Forget him, cousin, for heaven's sake! You know perfectly well that the rascal was seen three times in conversation with my brother-in-law's step-daughter, in consequence of which he should have married her. Now he has dropped the poor girl and left her the talk of the town.

FRAU STAAR. Yes, but for the love of God, whom *shall* we invite?

FRAU MORGENROTH. Here comes cousin Sperling.

(Enter Sperling with a large bouquet of flowers) [14]

SPERLING. Frau Deputy Collector of the Revenue—Frau Timber and Fishery Administrator—Frau City Excise-Office Recorder—your obedient servant. I was in my garden—Herr Vice-Churchwarden Staar sent the townhall messenger to me—I ran like a sunbeam, barely taking the time to pick these children of the spring.

THE THREE WOMEN. You know what happened?

SPERLING. I know everything. A famous scholar—coach turned over—nasal bone squashed—a letter of introduction from the ministry—

FRAU STAAR. Did you say a scholar?

FRAU BRENDEL. Nothing but a scholar?

FRAU MORGENROTH. And my delicious coffee in the fire!

FRAU STAAR. Don't you believe it, cousin. I've been told all my life that statesmen pay mighty little attention to scholars. No, no. This is a different case.

SPERLING. And I maintain that the man with the broken nose is a scholar recently arrived from Egypt or Weimar, who either measured the Sphinx or saw Herr von Goethe[21] looking out the window. In short, we've no time to lose. I brought the flowers. You, if you please, rush the children out to me. I *must* have children. Then let him come and see how things are done in Piffelheim.

FRAU STAAR. I'll bring them out. *(Exit)*

(Sperling practices his reception to one side)

---

[20] Literally, "in her gray bodice and green apron." This would be the costume of a maid-servant or a farmgirl.

[21] Adapted—for wider accessibility—from Pompey's Column (which stood outside ancient Alexandria) and Wieland. For the latter, see note 5 for Act Four.

FRAU MORGENROTH. Did you notice, cousin, the ridiculous airs our elderly relation gives herself?

FRAU BRENDEL. Didn't I though! She's as puffed up as a lump of dough in the oven.

FRAU MORGENROTH. Ha! To think that her husband was a mere *Deputy Collector of the Revenue.*

FRAU BRENDEL. Who died in debt to the cashbox.

FRAU MORGENROTH. And what sort of dinner can we expect? Do you remember the roast two months ago? Utterly burned.

FRAU BRENDEL. And her appearance! I wonder what she'll wear?

FRAU MORGENROTH. She has only three dresses.

FRAU BRENDEL. True. The brown dress—

FRAU MORGENROTH. The white dress—

FRAU BRENDEL. And the silk dress with the loud print.

FRAU MORGENROTH. Which she had made the first time the Mayor presided over a baptism.

FRAU BRENDEL. Beg your pardon, dear. It was when the Vice-Churchwarden married his second wife.

FRAU MORGENROTH. Who was also a fool.

FRAU BRENDEL. That she was.

[15] (*Enter Frau Staar with little Ursula and Gottlieb*[22] *eating large slices of buttered bread*)

FRAU STAAR. Here are the children.

SPERLING. Hand them over.

FRAU STAAR. First, make a nice bow and shake hands with the ladies. So.

FRAU BRENDEL (*wiping the butter off her fingers*). Such darlings! God bless them.

FRAU MORGENROTH (*likewise*). They look exactly like their dear grandmother.

FRAU BRENDEL. Have they had the smallpox yet?

FRAU STAAR. Not yet. My son keeps wanting to have them inoculated.[23] But I won't stand for it. One mustn't try to do God's work for him.

FRAU MORGENROTH. People nowadays want to herd their children with cattle.

---

[22] The two children are not given their name and and sex until the third act. These brats contrast refreshingly with the little angels in Kotzebue's "serious" plays. We have met two of them in *Menschenhass* (see the introductory essay). In the *Hussiten vor Naumburg* mentioned in note 15, a whole procession of these heart-breaking tots, crying "Mercy, mercy!" save the town from the terrible Prokop. ("Détestable pièce. 60 enfants à la fois sur le théatre," Benjamin Constant noted in his diary in Weimar in 1804.)

[23] Edward Jenner had performed his first inoculation against the small-pox in 1796. Vaccination was still very much in the news at the time our play was written. The two ladies are well informed at any rate regarding the source of the serum.

FRAU BRENDEL. Yes, they draw their stuff from the beasts in the field.

FRAU STAAR. Oh, it's a godless, bestial business.

SPERLING (*who has been busying himself with the children*). Children, put your bread away, it's full of butter.

THE CHILDREN. No! No!

SPERLING. Well then, use your clean hand for the flowers.

(*Enter Herr Staar hurriedly*)

[16]

HERR STAAR. He's going through the town gate this very moment. The street is full of little boys running alongside the carriage and gaping into his face.

(*Enter the Mayor likewise*)

MAYOR. He's coming! He's coming! The watchman is downstairs with his bugle.

SPERLING. Oh no! The children aren't ready; they'll look stupid—

HERR STAAR. Just throw the flowers about. Throw them at his face.

(*Enter Lotte likewise*)

LOTTE (*aside*). Olmers! Olmers is here!

(*The bugle blows out of tune*)

MAYOR. *Allons!* Let's meet him.

HERR STAAR. The children first!

SPERLING (*tearing the bread out of their hands and throwing it on the table*). The bread stays here till later.

HERR STAAR (*pushing the children through the door*). Forward, march!

THE CHILDREN (*screaming*). My bread! My bread!

MAYOR (*following them out*). Will you shut up!

(*Exeunt Sperling and Herr Staar. Lotte throws kisses through the window*)

FRAU STAAR. Frau Timber and Fishery Administrator, will you be so kind as to precede us?

FRAU BRENDEL. Not on my life. Frau City Excise-Office Recorder, I beg you—

FRAU MORGENROTH. Frau Deputy Collector of the Revenue, the honor belongs to you.

FRAU STAAR. Heaven forbid! I am in my own house.

FRAU BRENDEL. I know my obligations—

FRAU MORGENROTH. I *will* not budge. (*All three talk at once as the curtain falls*).

ACT 2

[1]   *The three women are still at the door making assaults of courtesy. Lotte stands to one side.*

FRAU BRENDEL. You must excuse me—
FRAU MORGENROTH. I beg to decline—
FRAU STAAR. Please do not lead me into temptation.
FRAU BRENDEL. Oh, I hear them coming up the stairs.
[2]   (*All three spring back as Olmers, the Mayor, Herr Staar, and Sperling enter*)
MAYOR. Blessed is my house. Blessed is our beloved Piffelheim.
OLMERS. Not so, Herr Mayor. I shall be very happy (*looking at Lotte*) if but a single person rejoices at my arrival.
MAYOR. God forbid! Don't let me catch any of our citizens refusing to humbly rejoice. We have our methods.
OLMERS. I take it that these ladies are members of your family?
MAYOR. Our distinguished neighbor, Widow Timber and Fishery Administrator Brendel and Widow City Excise-Office Recorder Morgenroth.
FRAU BRENDEL and FRAU MORGENROTH (*with tremendous curtsies*). We are deeply gratified by the honor—
MAYOR. And this is my mother, Frau Deputy Collector of the Revenue Staar.
FRAU STAAR. I make a thousand apologies for the unwashed curtains. Our custom is to clean them twice a year, before Whitsuntide and Christmas.
OLMERS. Ah, Frau Staar, I couldn't forgive myself if I were the cause of any alteration in your accustomed ways.
FRAU STAAR (*aside, offended*). Frau Staar? Is that all?
OLMERS (*to the Mayor*). This young lady, I suppose, is your daughter.
MAYOR. Everybody realizes it right away because of the resemblance.
OLMERS. Miss Staar, may I entertain the hope that my presence is not wholly unwelcome to you?
LOTTE. You may. Indeed, I should have been happy to welcome it *sooner*.
HERR STAAR. You can tell right away that the girl has spent a year in the capital.
OLMERS. I fancy that you made some interesting acquaintances there.
LOTTE. Not many perhaps. But *one* certainly.
OLMERS. Who must feel lucky indeed.
LOTTE. Who knows? One finds a little bit of everything in our capital, except memory.
OLMERS. Beware. These words may be unjust and you may come to regret them.
LOTTE. I shall be happy if I do.

OLMERS. Whoever has had the good fortune to gaze at you—

LOTTE. You're flattering a poor country girl.

MAYOR. Now, now, Lottchen, you're hardly a country girl. We live, thank heaven, in a city of some consequence.

HERR STAAR. Both our main streets are paved.

SPERLING. Five thousand inhabitants, among them several poets.

FRAU BRENDEL. A delightful promenade to the gallows.

OLMERS. I noticed some lovely high grounds.

FRAU MORGENROTH. Simply perfect for drying out the wash.

OLMERS. And a most picturesque vale sprinkled with bushes.

FRAU BRENDEL. Where you find the best strawberries.

SPERLING (*with a knowing look at Lotte*). As purple-red and aromatic as certain lips.

OLMERS. A river snakes its way at the bottom.

FRAU STAAR. Full of trout and carp.

OLMERS. A shady wood invites a host of nightingales.

HERR STAAR. The wood is dense enough and yet every year the price of timber rises.

OLMERS. Does your little town enjoy some flourishing trade?

FRAU STAAR. Oh yes, in horse-radish.

HERR STAAR. We also possess an establishment dealing in East- and West-Indian spices,[1] together with a circulating library.

SPERLING. I suppose you *have* heard of our target-practice range.

OLMERS. Alas, I haven't.

SPERLING. With a Jack Pudding who beats the drum for every bull's eye.[2]

FRAU STAAR. And we have an afternoon preacher[3] at St. Giles—an apostle of a man! Surely you've heard of him?

---

[1] Staar has something to boast about. A provincial town of about 5000 inhabitants had, typically, no shops at all in our sense of the word except for the one emporium selling "colonial wares," that is to say, all the groceries and dry-goods which people did not produce themselves, or could not purchase from local producers like butchers and bakers and travelling retailers.

[2] In the original, Sperling says, "A Hanswurst goes with it too" or "It includes a Hanswurst." Hanswurst was and is the German avatar of Arlecchino, Jack Pudding, or Punch. I have him beat on a drum in order to avoid puzzling today's audience. Kotzebue's audience would presumably have known what the Hanswurst was really doing at the target-range. Kotzebue himself provides the information in chapter 16 of his Italian travel book (1805): "When I was at Innsbruck, it happened that the Emperor's name-day was being celebrated. The citizens had organized a target-practice event, and I had occasion to admire the famous skill of the Tyrolean marksmen. . . . At least eight out of ten or twelve hit the bull's eye every time. As a result, the Hanswurst (who, as is customary, had to step forward after every shot and point to the place struck by the bullet) felt so sure that no one would fire to the side, that he often remained standing *next* to the target [rather than behind it?]. He must have been confident not only in the skill, but also in the sobriety of his countrymen."

[3] The afternoon preacher would be a *Hilfsprediger*, i.e. an assistant to the pastor; hence the humor in this passage. It is a fair guess that Kotzebue's audience would imagine him as a young man— probably an ordained minister awaiting his first benefice—not unlikely to cause an innocent flutter in a pious lady's heart.

OLMERS. The fact, I'm ashamed to—

SPERLING. And what do they say about our amateur theatricals? I play the fool in Kotzebue's *Hatred and Remorse*.[4]

FRAU MORGENROTH. And so naturally, too.

SPERLING. I do, don't I?

MAYOR. Before anything else I mean to show the gentleman our townhall. An architect from the city of Gotha built it three hundred years ago; so it's done in the true Gothic taste.[5]

OLMERS. As soon as I've recovered a bit from my journey.

FRAU STAAR. Lottchen, show the gentleman to his room.

LOTTE. With all my heart.

MAYOR. And I shall have the honor of escorting you.

HERR STAAR. So will I.

SPERLING. And so will I.

OLMERS. Please don't trouble yourselves, gentlemen; I'm perfectly happy with my guide.

MAYOR. Out of the question. Inasmuch as His Excellency, the Prime Minister has placed your distinguished self in my care, I propose to follow you like your own shadow.

OLMERS. This means you will keep coming between me and the sun.

MAYOR. As much sun as you like. Your window, sir, faces the south. Altogether comfortable quarters. A mere three steps down into the room and again two steps up to the four-poster in the alcove.

OLMERS (*taking Lotte's hand*). Mademoiselle, with your helping hand, I hope that climbing those steps will be easy.

LOTTE. Better if we had reached our destination by now.

(*Exits with Olmers, followed by the Mayor*).

SPERLING (*to Herr Staar*). What do you think? Shall I read him my Ode right now? The one to our Piffelheimer Ale?[6]

HERR STAAR. Not now. First, I want to show him my prints of famous sieges

---

[4] Some of the best scenes in *Menschenhass und Reue* involve a young dolt named Peter. Kotzebue often flattered himself by needling his own sentimental plays in his comedies, and *Menschenhass*, the most famous of them all, in particular.

[5] Needless to say, the Thuringian town of Gotha is not responsible for the Gothic style. We note here, and will again, Kotzebue's resistance to the Romantic admiration of medieval Germany—a somewhat loose term, inasmuch as it takes in the sixteenth century and includes such figures as Luther, Dürer, Hans Sachs, Faust—and the distinctly pre-classical architecture then prevalent. Not so incidentally, Berlin was a center of neo-classicism, both spiritually and visibly in its architecture and urban design.

[6] Adapted from Sperling's Ode to *Die Braunschweiger Mumme*, namely a thick brown beer from Brunswick. According to Lombard, it was named after a gentleman named Mumme who began to produce it in 1492.

and battles.[7] (*Exeunt*)

FRAU STAAR. Well, what do you say, my dear cousins? [3]

FRAU BRENDEL. He hardly so much as looked at me.

FRAU MORGENROTH. He didn't speak a word to me.

FRAU STAAR. And he called me plain Frau Staar. Can you believe it? I thank my stars I am Frau Deputy Collector of the Revenue and no plain Frau Staar.

FRAU BRENDEL. He could have asked me whether my husband died a long time ago or something in that vein.

FRAU MORGENROTH. At the very least, he might have asked after my children.

FRAU STAAR. My son said to him distinctly enough: Frau Deputy Collector of the Revenue; and yet he shamelessly called me Frau Staar.

FRAU MORGENROTH. We'll have to teach him manners here in Piffelheim.

FRAU BRENDEL. He's a pretty fellow, though.

FRAU STAAR. Yes, but wanting in that nice touch of stiffness. I thought he behaved as if he were in his own home.

FRAU MORGENROTH. How true! He didn't seem a bit embarrassed.

FRAU BRENDEL. Still, he was wearing a fine shirt.

FRAU STAAR. Without frills on his cuffs.[8]

FRAU MORGENROTH. As for his hair, I've a suspicion that it's been a week since it was last powdered.[9]

FRAU STAAR. Somehow the man looks familiar to me. I keep feeling I've seen him somewhere before. (*Suddenly*) Oh, oh! I'm dizzy. I'm going to faint.

---

[7] In the original, Herr Staar speaks only of his Nürnberg prints. I assume that he owns a collection of popular sixteenth- and seventeenth-century woodcuts published in that center of single-leaf woodcut art. Today we spontaneously think of Albrecht Dürer in this connection, but most Nürnberg prints were humble and crude pictures, intended for the "mass market." Their subject matter included the sieges and battles I have Staar mention, religious themes, portraits of kings and heroes, sensational occurrences of the two-headed calf variety, and astronomical, astrological, and meteorological subjects. In any event, Nürnberg, having remained nearly intact as a medieval town, became a focus of Romantic enthusiasm after Tieck and Wachenroder "discovered" it during a famous journey south in 1793. But Kotzebue was not the man for ancient crooked streets, church-spires, venerable tryptichs, or picturesque townhalls. As a result, the normal modern reader finds himself siding with the victims of the satire, and against the satirist, for who does not (nowadays) prefer gabled half-timbered houses to imitations of Greek temples? But this should no more "invalidate" Kotzebue for us than our disagreements with unassailable writers. Who sides with Molière today when he preaches that women ought to stay home and attend to their pots and pans?

[8] In the original, Frau Staar complains that Olmers displays no cuffs at all. Costume illustrations show that around 1790 men's cuffs still made a separate show beyond the sleeves of the jacket. Around 1800 the cuffs seem to have retreated into the sleeves.

[9] For the Berlin audience in 1802, the humor—requiring no footnote—would derive from the fact that Olmers naturally does not powder his hair at all. Wigs, as has been mentioned before, had been on their way out since the French Revolution. Thereafter Bonaparte gave up powdering his hair and allowed it to appear in its natural color. This was the beginning of the end of powder for masculine manes throughout Europe.

FRAU BRENDEL and FRAU MORGENROTH (*sustaining her*). What is it?

FRAU STAAR. There—in my pocket—

FRAU BRENDEL. The smelling salts?

FRAU STAAR. No—no—a portrait—a portrait—

FRAU BRENDEL. Here it is. Oh dear, it's the stranger!

FRAU STAAR. Let me look at it. The very man, as I hope to be saved, the
    very man! I won't survive it! (*She sinks into a chair*)

FRAU BRENDEL. Who is it?

FRAU MORGENROTH. I hope he's not—

FRAU STAAR. I can't talk—

FRAU BRENDEL. He's not an escaped convict, is he?

FRAU MORGENROTH. Very likely. They're probably circulating his picture
    along with a description.

FRAU STAAR. He's the King!

BOTH (*screaming*). The King!

FRAU STAAR. His glorious Majesty!

FRAU BRENDEL. Cousin, I feel faint.

(*She sinks into another chair*)

FRAU MORGENROTH. And so do I.

(*Sinks into yet another chair*)

(*All three groan*)

FRAU STAAR. No, I won't survive this—so much honor—such high favor—
    and the curtains unwashed—

FRAU BRENDEL. No one in town is aware—?

FRAU STAAR. Not a soul.

FRAU BRENDEL. Ah! This means I must hurry. Are you coming, cousin?

FRAU MORGENROTH. Yes, I am, though I feel as if I had lead in my feet—
    but the King—our patriotic duty—let's go!—let's go!

(*Exeunt both*)

[4] FRAU STAAR (*alone*). I'm in a daze—but never mind—now whenever
    Heaven wills it, let my last hour strike. Yes, now in God's name, I am wil-
    ling to be plain Frau Staar. Let the King call me Frau Staar as often as he
    pleases. Hark! he is walking back and forth upstairs—so obviously a
    royal footstep! If only I could move out of this chair—if I could inform
    my son—so he won't make some horrid faux pas—

[5] (*Enter the Mayor, Herr Staar, and Sperling*)

FRAU STAAR. Are you here at last? Look at me. Here I sit and who knows
    whether I'll ever get up again.

MAYOR. What has happened to you, mother?

FRAU STAAR. I want to be brief—I want to speak—I want to unburden
    myself of the great secret—and then I want to go into my little room and
    sing a hymn of praise at the top of my voice.

HERR STAAR. Mother, whatever are you babbling about?

FRAU STAAR. Where is your guest?

SPERLING. He'll be coming down in a minute.

FRAU STAAR. Is anyone with him?

MAYOR. Not a soul. Lotte wanted to stay with him but I chased her into the kitchen.

FRAU STAAR. Then run! Sweep up the stairs on your knees. Nicholas, Nicholas, the King is in your house!

MAYOR and HERR STAAR. Who? What?

SPERLING. The King?

MAYOR. Please, mother, don't muddle my head.

FRAU STAAR. The muddle hasn't even begun. All Piffelheim will be in a muddle. He's here, I tell you. He's here! Like the great King of the World who rode into Jerusalem on an ass. He has chosen you, my son Nicholas. He has taken up his abode in *your* house, you lucky Mayor, also Senior Church Elder.

MAYOR. Dearest mother, will you kindly explain yourself—because I can no longer tell whether I've a head or a windmill sitting on my shoulders.

FRAU STAAR. Here! Here is the portrait of our gracious King. Look for yourselves. Is it himself or isn't it?

MAYOR. The stranger as he lives and breathes!

HERR STAAR. Exactly. But mother, how do you know—

FRAU STAAR. Didn't I see the King's grandfather forty years ago?[10] And isn't the grandson his spitting image? I tell you it's his portrait, and the hallowed creature is walking above our heads.

HERR STAAR. I have it! He's traveling incognito.

SPERLING. The father of our nation in the stone-pit!

MAYOR. Oh my God! What's to be done now? The civic guard has to be drawn up with the old drum.

SPERLING. And the Piffelheimer Marksmen with their banner.

HERR STAAR. And the town council with the orphans.

FRAU STAAR. Oh, if my husband, may he rest in peace, had lived to see this day!

MAYOR. But are you really sure?

STAAR. Brother, how can you doubt it? Mother saw the grandfather with her own eyes.

SPERLING. And you can't exactly disprove the portrait.

FRAU STAAR. It's the King, I tell you!

MAYOR. All right then, all the bells must be rung to summon the citizenry.

FRAU STAAR. Frau Brendel and Frau Morgenroth are spreading the news.

[10] The grandfather of Frederick William III was Prince August Wilhelm, brother to Frederick the Great. It may well be that the theater audience of the day would picture, in the fugitive instant this line was spoken, the memorable monarch rather than the more or less forgotten brother.

MAYOR. Then the bells won't be needed. But a guard of honor must be posted
at once before the house.

FRAU STAAR. Before *our* house! When I see that guard of honor I'll burst a
blood vessel and die.

SPERLING. Here he comes.

FRAU STAAR (*manages to rise from her chair*). Oh God, oh God!

MAYOR. Courage.

[6]   (*Enter Olmers*)

OLMERS. A most comfortable house, my dear Mayor, and a splendid view. I
hope to spend many happy hours here.

MAYOR. Your gracious Majesty—

OLMERS. Eh?

HERR STAAR. Your Royal Highness—

OLMERS. What?

SPERLING. Glorious monarch—

OLMERS. Is this some sort of joke?

FRAU STAAR. Anointed of the Lord—

OLMERS. What is this? April fool's day?[11]

MAYOR. Conceal yourself no longer from your loyal subjects.

FRAU STAAR. Our hearts are burning—

SPERLING. And blazing—

FRAU STAAR. And melting—

OLMERS. What are you people up to?

MAYOR. Your Highness's Prime Minister has more than hinted already—

OLMERS. My Prime Minister? (*Aside*) I seem to have landed in a lunatic
asylum.

[7]   (*Enter the maid*)

MAID. There are two men outside. They say they're delegated from the Piffelheimer Marksmen and want to welcome the King.

MAYOR. Will Your Majesty graciously allow them?

OLMERS. The devil I will! Are you mad? I'm no more a majesty than you're
a night watchman.

MAYOR. In God's name, why should your all-gracious Highness deny it any
longer? We have Your Majesty's priceless portrait in our possession.

OLMERS. My portrait?

FRAU STAAR. Here it is, almighty King.

OLMERS. Well yes, to be sure it *is* my portrait—

MAYOR. At last! (*To the maid*) Let the delegation enter. Let it be favored with
instant admission.

OLMERS. For God's sake, no. You'll only make a fool of me; my name is

[11] Kotzebue has "the sixth of January," that is to say, Epiphany (*Dreikönigstag*, the day of the three
kings), when the guest who found the bean in his cake became king for the occasion.

Karl Olmers, period.

HERR STAAR. Brother Nicholas, let be; His Majesty is making it plain that he wishes to remain incognito.

FRAU STAAR. But the guard of honor, Your Highness. Surely, you will not reject the guard of honor.

OLMERS. If you don't put a stop to this nonsense, I *will* need a guard, and no mistake, because I'm losing my sanity. (*To Lotte who has entered*) Ah, mademoiselle, I'm glad you are here. Your relations are compelling me to be the King. How this has happened God only knows. I'm no king and have no wish to rule over anything—except one particular heart. If I succeed in *that* I shall not envy any monarch. (*Exit*)

MAYOR. His Majesty must be accompanied. (*He wants to go*) [8]

LOTTE. (*stopping him*). Father, please explain—what does all this mean? How did you come to think—

MAYOR. Out of my way, Miss know-it-all. The man is our King.

LOTTE. God forbid! Where have you heard this nonsense?

HERR STAAR. Nonsense?

MAYOR. Didn't my mother see his grandfather once?

HERR STAAR. Hasn't she got his portrait?

FRAU STAAR. Which the girl herself gave me.

LOTTE. Oh, now I understand—good heavens, I was only joking!

ALL. Joking?

LOTTE. Forgive me, dearest granny—

FRAU STAAR. I'll twist your head about your neck!

LOTTE. How could I guess—

FRAU STAAR. You God-forsaken girl. So then, you knew all along whose portrait it is.

LOTTE (*embarrassed*). No—that I didn't—

FRAU STAAR. How did it fall into your hands?

LOTTE. I—I found it.

FRAU STAAR. Found it? Where? How?

LOTTE. When I was in Berlin—taking a walk—I found it lying in the grass. I slipped it into my pocket and until today I'd forgotten all about it.

FRAU STAAR. Is that so! Then why were you mooning so tenderly over it when I came in this morning?

LOTTE. Tenderly?

FRAU STAAR. Yes, miss. Deaf and blind to the world.

SPERLING. What's this, Miss Lotte?[12]

---

[12] Olmers and Sperling both call Lotte "Mademoiselle," and her grandmother has just addressed her as "Mamsell," the contracted familiar form. As is well known, the German language was massively "invaded" by French, so that Kotzebue's audience would have made nothing in particular of the fact that both rivals use this gallicism. I have instead deprived Sperling and Frau Staar of it because for us, it would suggest genuine sophistication.

LOTTE. It's easy to explain. I was concentrating. A lost portrait had been advertised in the newspapers. I remembered the one I had found. I whipped it out of my pocket and was comparing it with the description in the article.

FRAU STAAR. I didn't see any newspapers.

LOTTE. They're lying on the table.

FRAU STAAR (*pulling out her spectacles*). Show me. I want to read the article myself.

LOTTE (*frightened*). Of course—why not—here you are—ah, what bad luck, just where the children put their buttered bread. It soaked right through—the paper's illegible.

FRAU STAAR. One trick after another! And what if I had pinned the portrait to my bonnet? I would have become the laughingstock of Piffelheim. Away with it! And don't let me ever see it again.

MAYOR. Return it to the stranger.[13]

LOTTE. Oh yes; otherwise he could imagine heaven knows what—

SPERLING. And leave the replacement to me. I shall have myself painted—

LOTTE (*aside*). Why not stuffed?

HERR STAAR. Niece, you're nothing but a fool. See how a twit of a girl can turn an entire respectable city topsy-turvy like her sewing box. I'd better go and quiet people down. (*Exit*)

MAYOR. And I'd better dismiss the delegation. One thing I'm telling you. You bring another such king into the house and you won't budge from your spinning-wheel again![14] (*Exit*)

[13] Jakob Minor (1911, p. 111) observes that the idea of Olmers' being mistaken for the King is strained, and one cannot help agreeing. Schumacher objects on structural gounds. According to him, the episode is a red herring: Kotzebue drops the matter, and it has no further bearing on the plot. In this respect, however, the episode can be defended. It strongly brings out Piffelheim's worship of titles—so dramatically that we now fully realize that Olmers' untitled nudity will be an insuperable obstacle. On the other hand, a more concrete authorial error has not attracted any attention. Surely by this time Lotte's relations, dim as they are, *must* have noticed the extreme unlikelihood that the portrait she claims to have found by accident in the grass in Berlin should have no connection with the visitor arriving with a letter of recommendation. Even they, in other words, must realize at this point that the two young persons know each other, and, as a result, the time is *now* for the grand revelation that Olmers has come to Piffelheim to ask for Lotte's hand. The error is plain—but, I suspect, deliberate. Kotzebue *will* very shortly produce the revelation. He merely wishes to postpone it so as to allow the supposed stranger to sink deeper into disgrace. Audiences and readers tend to forgive—or overlook—structural cracks of this sort.

[14] Literally, "I shall send you to the spinning-room." Bailly, Lombard, Guignard, and Schumacher all interpret *Spinnstube* as equivalent to *Spinnhaus*, that is to say, the workhouse for paupers and delinquents. Mathes does not comment. But surely Kotzebue meant the Mayor's threat to be credible to Lotte (and the audience), not "crazy." The punishment he invokes is similar to confining Lotte to her room on a meager diet—somewhat like the unhappy Clarissa Harlowe. It should be noted, in this connection, that a middle-class family in the provinces would as naturally perform its own spinning, weaving, and sewing as the cooking and baking already mentioned in the play. We also recall that Frau Staar has reminisced about her agreeable hours at the spinning-wheel while she was being courted. Fashionable Lotte is, instead, a gadabout, and her father knows that she is more likely to ask for another trip to Berlin than wool for her spinning-wheel.

FRAU STAAR. All this rejoicing for nothing. The honor guard at our door—the story to tell my departed on his grave—and in the meantime my roast is burned to ashes, you little wretch. (*Exit*)

LOTTE. Herr Assistant Inspector of Buildings, Roads, and Mines, I imagine [9] that you too have some business to attend to before dinner.

SPERLING. My dearest mademoiselle, whether before or after dinner I have no other business than wrapping you in my adoration.

LOTTE. Wrapping me? Like an overcoat?

SPERLING. Poetically speaking, my adoration *is* an overcoat, a garment with never a crease in it. Beautiful Lotte, try it out. It will keep you warm through storm and frost.

LOTTE. I'm still so young, sir, that I require no borrowed heat.

SPERLING. Perish the thought. My heart is not on loan. It is a gift. (*He kneels*) Here at your feet, receive your property. Dispose of it as you desire. The king has vanished, but the queen stands before me. *My* queen. My divinity.

(*Enter Olmers*) [10]

OLMERS (*startled*). I beg your pardon. Such a lovely interview mustn't be disturbed.

(*Sperling rises*)

LOTTE. There was nothing to it. Do come in.

OLMERS (*bitterly*). Nothing to it? For *some* people I can think of, there might be a great deal to what I've just seen.

SPERLING. And they wouldn't be mistaken. Let me inform you, sir, that after an eternity of two years, true love has conquered at last.

OLMERS. Really? My congratulations.

SPERLING. If you tarry a few weeks among us, you will attend a celebration at which Amor and Hymen are to be united in a brotherly embrace.

OLMERS. Indeed?

LOTTE. I myself wish it with all my heart.

OLMERS. Admirable frankness! I certainly shall stay till then—after all, I must have *some* compensation for my ruined carriage.

LOTTE. The truth is that I am not yet betrothed, but I hope to be before long.

OLMERS. Not yet betrothed? You're jesting, surely.

SPERLING. A delicious jest from a handmaiden to the Three Graces.

LOTTE. Understand me correctly, sir. I had hoped that my suitor would declare himself, but five weeks went by and he never said a word.

SPERLING. Never said a word? You tease. Didn't my eyes speak volumes?

OLMERS (*beginning to understand*). Perhaps he said nothing while he was preparing everything.

SPERLING. Exactly, sir. The carpenters are still working in my new lodgings. Meanwhile I am renting an attic from Herr Vice-Churchwarden Staar.

LOTTE. He *could* have sent news by a third hand.

SPERLING. But didn't I lie daily at your feet in person?

OLMERS. Perhaps he took too conscientiously a strict prohibition dictated by maidenly modesty.

SPERLING. A good guess, sir. When the young lady left for Berlin she gave me specific orders not to forward my sighs.

LOTTE. Some willing neighbor might have been employed.

SPERLING. Beautiful Lotte, all our neighbors are infernal gossips.

OLMERS. Besides, he may have felt that he had offered so many proofs of love and fidelity that he had won the right to be fully trusted.

SPERLING. A palpable hit, sir. I am as faithful as a poodle.[15]

LOTTE. Do you really believe, Herr Olmers, that my lover's feelings are as warm today as they were in the past?

SPERLING. What warm? Boiling hot! Yes, mademoiselle, if Archimedes had felt such love, he wouldn't have needed that mirror of his catching the sun to set fire to the enemy's fleet.[16]

OLMERS. I dare affirm that this absence has but intensified his feelings.

SPERLING. And how! I nearly went berserk while she was away.

LOTTE. Well then, my mind's at rest again.

SPERLING. At last!

OLMERS. And so is mine.

SPERLING. How very charming of you, sir, to have worried yourself on my behalf. Allow me to look on you as my friend.

OLMERS. Your obedient servant.

LOTTE. Still, whoever loves me honorably will surely want certain others to be told.

SPERLING. What others?

OLMERS. It may be presumed that he will declare himself to your father.

SPERLING. All taken care of, sir.

LOTTE. Whatever remains to be done had better be done quickly, inasmuch as my engagement is set for tomorrow.

SPERLING. Precisely for this reason, nothing remains to be done.

OLMERS. But *if* something is still required, it will surely be taken care of this very evening.

SPERLING. Of course.

[15] In the original, Sperling alludes to "Melai's dog in Meissner's *Sketches*"—a reference Mathes corrects by naming another work, namely A. G. Meissner's *Erzählungen und Dialogen* (Stories and Dialogues, 1781, second edition 1790). The tale concerns a king of Hindustan betrayed by all who loved him, left on the road as a starving wanderer, and saved from death when the only creature who has stood by him, his dog, brings him an edible rabbit *in extremis*. While Kotzebue aims a few shafts at his enemies, he also gracefully nods towards his friends: Wieland, Engel, and here Meissner, who had written him a tactful letter of support during the infamous Bahrdt affair (Kotzebue 1821, p. 305-6).

[16] To wit, at the siege of Syracuse by the Romans in 214-212 B.C.

LOTTE. I sway between hope and fear.

SPERLING. Throw yourself cheerfully into the arms of hope.

OLMERS. A persuasive advocate might be helpful.

SPERLING. Whatever for? We have the family's consent:
> The butterfly and rose shall make a twosome
> As he doth lap the dew out of her bosom.

LOTTE. So be it. In this gentleman's presence, I swear once more eternal love.

OLMERS. I accept the oath in your lover's name.

SPERLING. I'm melting away.

LOTTE. No power on earth shall part me from him.

OLMERS. He is bound to you forever and ever.

SPERLING. Now I'm crying.

LOTTE. I offer my hand to seal the oath.

OLMERS. I press it gratefully to my lips.

SPERLING. Oh, I'm so happy.

(Enter Frau Staar) [11]

FRAU STAAR. Dinner is ready. Our guests are waiting in the dining room. Will you be so very kind—

OLMERS. At your service, madam.

(He reaches Lotte's hand behind Sperling's back, and slips out with her)

SPERLING *(putting on a pair of white gloves)*. Triumphantly holding my bride's hand, I shall—*(he makes a courtly turn toward Lotte but finds himself in front of the grandmother)*

FRAU STAAR *(curtsying)*. Herr Assistant Inspector of Buildings, Roads, and Mines—

SPERLING *(stammering)*. Frau Deputy Collector of the Revenue—

(They take each other by the fingertips and he leads her out with a sweet-sour face)

ACT 3

[1]   FRAU STAAR (*alone*). Upon my soul, such impudence is more than I've ever experienced. So *these* are the good manners of the capital! God preserve us! The "Frau Staar" business I won't even mention anymore—I've swallowed that one and some day I may digest it. But—I show him the place of honor between two respectable old ladies and what does he do? He turns his back on them as if they were a pair of wax dummies at the fairground, and plunges into the crowd of young people! Well, well, well. Give me our Assistant Inspector of Buildings, Roads, and Mines any day. A real gentleman, a charmer, so neat, so trim.

[2]   (*Enter Frau Brendel and Frau Morgenroth, each decked out in her own way*)

FRAU STAAR. Well, cousin, what do you say? Our dear modest guest!

FRAU BRENDEL. A young scamp if ever I saw one.

FRAU MORGENROTH. Did you notice how he made bread pellets and threw them at your granddaughter?

FRAU STAAR. God's own bread. Can you believe such wickedness?

FRAU BRENDEL. He spilled the red wine on the tablecloth.

FRAU MORGENROTH. That's nothing. He almost burned a hole in it while trimming the light.

FRAU STAAR. The villain. My damask tablecloth.

FRAU BRENDEL. And I don't think he liked the food very much.

FRAU MORGENROTH. He didn't touch several of the dishes. What kind of behavior is *that*?

FRAU STAAR. It's not as if I didn't tell him over and over how tasteful all the dishes were, and what ingredients went into each.

FRAU BRENDEL. No one can deny that we all kept urging him to eat.

FRAU MORGENROTH. And he had the effrontery to ask us to stop.

FRAU STAAR. One can tell he's not accustomed to polite society.

FRAU BRENDEL. He didn't even praise the cake, that simply superb cake.

FRAU MORGENROTH. Ever so moist.

FRAU BRENDEL. It melted in one's mouth.

FRAU MORGENROTH. You baked it yourself, of course.

FRAU STAAR. Thank you; I did.

FRAU BRENDEL. I thought so right away.

FRAU STAAR. You're too kind.

FRAU MORGENROTH. The dough was like a froth.

FRAU STAAR. Hush—you're embarrassing me.

FRAU BRENDEL. May I ask how many eggs you required?

FRAU STAAR. Allow me to share the complete recipe with you. First you take—

(Enter Herr Staar) [3]

HERR STAAR. You can keep your distinguished guest. Or else, let him start with a book of etiquette from my circulating library and study it for a few days.

FRAU BRENDEL. You're so right, Herr Vice-Churchwarden. The man's education has been sorely neglected.

HERR STAAR. He couldn't so much as say grace without fumbling.

FRAU STAAR. Instead, he laughed at the poor children, although they got through their "For what we are about to receive" without a slip.

HERR STAAR. And when I brought out my merry old toast, "To those we love," he exclaimed, "And who love us in return," and gave his neighbor a kiss.

FRAU BRENDEL *(fanning herself coyly)*. It was my bad luck to sit on his left.

FRAU STAAR. Our pretty Miss Morgenroth, who sat on his right, became red hot.

HERR STAAR. Lotte threw him a ferocious look!

FRAU STAAR. To conclude, he wanted to sing a heathenish song about "Joy, gift of the gods"![1] No, sir, that sort of wickedness is not for *us*.

HERR STAAR. Because he has no title of his own, he won't give anyone else the one *he* has earned.

FRAU STAAR. While my son, the Mayor, also Senior Church Elder, was discoursing on his most important legal cases, he sat there scratching his plate with his fork.

FRAU BRENDEL. And the sugar he poured into his coffee, a fist-full of it.

FRAU MORGENROTH. And instead of kissing our cousin's hand after dinner, he bowed once roundabout and that was that.

HERR STAAR. What I'd like to know is how His Excellency can recommend such people.

(Enter Sperling) [4]

SPERLING. Oh, my cousins, I wish the stranger were still lying in the stone-pit, because between you and me, the man has no *savoir-faire*.

HERR STAAR. There we all agree.

SPERLING. Did you notice his superior smile when I suggested a game of charades?[2]

HERR STAAR. As for your lovely Ode to Piffelheim Malt, I don't think he heard three words of it.

---

[1] Schiller's famous "Ode to Joy" (set to music by Beethoven in his Ninth Symphony) which, according to Mathes, had become downright popular since its publication in 1787. In light of Kotzebue's little maneuvers in Weimar (see the introductory essay), it is probably no accident that the young hero sings Schiller while the fool quotes Goethe. See note 6.

[2] In the original, Sperling has proposed a *Leberreim* (liver-rhyme), a dinner-time game in which the person who has received the liver of the fish on his plate starts a line of verse with "This liver is from a . . . and not a . . ."; the other guests then continue *extempore* on the same rhyme.

FRAU BRENDEL. Instead, he kept winking at Miss Lotte who was sitting across the table from him.

SPERLING. He seems to be dead to good literature.

HERR STAAR. He hasn't read a single best-seller.[3]

SPERLING. Poor fellow. He may have the aptitude, but the trouble is: no education.

HERR STAAR. No breeding.

FRAU BRENDEL. No morality.

FRAU MORGENROTH. No social graces.

FRAU STAAR. No title.

SPERLING. Mark my words. If he shows up at tomorrow's celebration, the very children will laugh in his face.

HERR STAAR. Let us thank Heaven that here in our good Piffelheim, we know how to bring up our youngsters.

[5]   (*Enter Lotte*)

FRAU STAAR. I'm glad you came in, Lottchen. Tell us, do the young Berliners all resemble this Monsieur Olmers?

LOTTE. All the cultivated ones do.

FRAU STAAR. Is that so? Charming.

HERR STAAR. The man's a peasant, I tell you.

FRAU BRENDEL. Makes bread pellets.

FRAU MORGENROTH. Dirties tablecloths.

FRAU STAAR. Addresses people without their titles.

SPERLING. Ridicules poetry.

FRAU BRENDEL. Doesn't praise the cake.

FRAU MORGENROTH. Leaves half of it on his plate.

HERR STAAR. Knows nothing about grace at table.

FRAU STAAR. Wants to sing heathenish songs.

SPERLING. Kisses his neighbor.

FRAU STAAR. Doesn't pay attention to your father, nor to the pastor.

LOTTE. Woe, woe to poor Olmers! Dear grandmother, in the capital we try to be as unconstrained as possible. We know that compliments are as tiresome to those who pay them as to those who receive them. People eat what they like and how much they like. No one keeps urging them. Prayers are omitted at table because the children merely babble and the grownups pay no heed to them. A harmless joke or a merry song adds spice to the meal. As for titles, they are kept for official occasions; at a party they would spoil everybody's enjoyment. In short, a good host tries to remove every possible impediment to well-being. His guests come and

---

[3] In the original, "He has not even read *Rinaldo Rinaldini*." Goethe's brother-in-law, Christian August Vulpius, was the author of this recently published and very popular tale of robbers, which Kotzebue pointedly despised. Naturally, Goethe wanted him to excise this passage in the play.

go, sit down, stand up, and take their leave as the spirit moves them, without ceremony.[4]

FRAU STAAR. Stop. One of my dizzy spells is coming on.

FRAU BRENDEL. Without saying goodbye? Is that possible?

FRAU MORGENROTH. Not to say thank you for the honor?

LOTTE. The best thank-you for the host is to see his guests enjoying themselves.

FRAU STAAR. God almighty! Has our capital become a village tavern?

(*Enter the Mayor and Olmers*)   [6]

MAYOR. As I was saying, Herr Olmers, for a hundred years the Piffelheim herd has enjoyed the privilege of grazing in the stubble-fields of Rummelsburg—

OLMERS. And so—?

MAYOR. This didn't prevent their bailiff from seizing one of our sheep recently—

OLMERS (*to Lotte*). My pretty young hostess slipped away from me.

MAYOR. I said, he seized one of our sheep—

OLMERS. Though your household duties dress you in a thousand charms.

MAYOR. I said a fat sheep—

LOTTE (*aside to Olmers*). Pay attention to the sheep, will you!

OLMERS. Enough, Herr Mayor. You have given me a surplus of evidence for the privilege of the Piffelheim herd. It's clear as daylight that the bailiff must restitute the sheep.

MAYOR. To be sure; but that's not the end of it.

OLMERS. He must be fined as well, as heavily as you like. (*To Frau Staar*) Don't you agree, Madam? You have feasted us so beautifully that for the moment even the fattest of sheep cannot arouse our interest.

FRAU STAAR. It is my general impression, sir, that sensible conversation doesn't arouse *everybody's* interest. In my day, however, one's elders were venerated. Titled persons who had reached the years of discretion spoke, untitled youth listened and learned. Inasmuch as this honorable custom has fallen into disuse, the elderly had better withdraw from society and mourn over our moral decay in Christian solitude. (*She bows and leaves*)

OLMERS. The lady is not angry with *me*, I hope.

HERR STAAR. My mother, the Frau Deputy Collector of the Revenue, enjoys such high regard in all of Piffelheim that she can feel no anger, even when

[4] Frederick William III was almost a bourgeois ruler, and high society in Berlin had become, if not informal in the American sense, at any rate vastly less "Prussian" than what the word suggests to our minds. Lotte seems to be describing the ambience of one of the brilliant *salons*—several were presided over by wealthy Jewesses—which helped make of Berlin a remarkable and notably tolerant intellectual center after the reign of Frederick the Great and before the collapse of Prussia in 1805.

this or that individual deprives her of the title which is her due. (*Exits*)

OLMERS. Good heavens. These provincial titles are so long and to study them is such a bore—

SPERLING. Especially if one hasn't one oneself. (*Exits*)

OLMERS. There ought to be no stodginess in merry company.

FRAU BRENDEL. Since one attends a banquet, not in order to be merry, but in order to partake of God's plenty with decorous enjoyment, decency requires that one give the respective dignities of the assembled company their due. (*She bows and leaves*)

FRAU MORGENROTH. Particularly so, because upon the decencies of Ceremony depends the purity of the Moral Law. (*Likewise*)

OLMERS. God forbid!

MAYOR (*aside, adjusting his wig*). I'd tell him off too if it weren't for His Excellency.

LOTTE (*aside to Olmers*). You're doing everything to antagonize the whole family. Go talk to my father before it's too late. (*Exits*)

[7]   MAYOR. To return to the sheep I was telling you about—

OLMERS. My dear Herr Mayor! Though you might promise me all the sheep of Tibet, I have a desire just now that lies closer to my heart.

MAYOR. Oh?

OLMERS. I love your daughter.

MAYOR. Well, well.

OLMERS. I want to marry her.

MAYOR. Honored, I'm sure.

OLMERS. I possess a sufficient fortune, and thanks to the Minister's good will I hope shortly to secure a respectable place in the administration.

MAYOR. Congratulations.

OLMERS. All I need to complete my happiness is your consent. May I flatter myself that—?

MAYOR. Your obedient servant.

OLMERS. I have presented my request like an honest man, in few, unadorned words. Pray answer me likewise.

MAYOR. To be sure. However, with your permission—I am the *pater familias*—my duty requires that I summon a council of my relations and submit your petition in suitable *terminis*.

OLMERS. Do so. In the meantime I shall take a turn around the garden and wait impatiently for your decision. (*Exits*)

[8]   MAYOR (*alone*). Will you look at this! The man all but breaks down my door! Is that how one gets married? Doesn't he know that a young suitor has to spend half a year visiting the family, in and out of the house at decent intervals so it becomes the talk of the town, before arriving at these finalities? God forgive me the sinful thought—but this now would look as though we had to drum the girl to the altar for certain reasons. (*He goes to*

the door and calls) Margaret! Tell the whole company to join me at once; I've something of high importance to consider with them. (*To himself*) Hey ho, if it weren't for the Minister, I'd have sent the lad packing on the spot. But as I'd dearly like to have him give a full account of tomorrow's celebration to His Excellency, I must handle him with kid gloves.

(*Enter Frau Staar, Herr Staar, Frau Brendel, and Frau Morgenroth*)　　[9]

FRAU MORGENROTH. Herr Mayor, you called us and here we are.

FRAU STAAR. What is your wish, my son?

HERR STAAR. What do you want, brother?

MAYOR. A consultation on a family matter is in order; and so I wanted to call my loving relations together.

FRAU BRENDEL and FRAU MORGENROTH. What's happened, cousin? Tell us!

MAYOR. A brand-new event.

FRAU BRENDEL. Nothing to do, I hope, with that wife of the new Tax Collector, who was determined to push herself ahead of our dear old cousin at communion?

FRAU STAAR. Let her try.

MAYOR. No, that's not it.

FRAU MORGENROTH. Or with the surgeon's boy, who called your little Gottlieb a blockhead?

MAYOR. No, that affair has gone before the town council and will take at least two years to settle.

FRAU STAAR. In that case, explain what it's all about, my son.

MAYOR. First let us sit down so we can proceed in an orderly manner—my mother, as head of the family, in the middle, her immediate lineage to the right and left of her, and on either flank, our cousins. So.

(*Everyone sits down*)

FRAU BRENDEL. I'm dying to hear!

FRAU MORGENROTH. I'm bursting to know!

MAYOR (*clearing his throat*). It is familiar knowledge to all present that the oldest daughter born to me in wedlock, Lotte by name, has reached a marriageable age.

FRAU STAAR. Of course, and that is why she's getting married.

FRAU BRENDEL. Though *some* might think her a bit too young.

FRAU MORGENROTH. And a bit too saucy, I'd say, if she weren't my dear relation.

HERR STAAR. I agree. The books in my circulating library aren't good enough for her anymore.

FRAU BRENDEL. And *rather* worldly; she has all the new fashions sent her from Berlin.

FRAU MORGENROTH. A while ago she made free to joke about our way of making a curtsy.

FRAU BRENDEL. Though our old dancing master was a celebrity in his day.

FRAU MORGENROTH. To be sure, he knew nothing about the new hopsasa.

FRAU BRENDEL. And didn't tolerate anyone's lifting up her long skirt like a wet rag in order to go walking in the street.

FRAU STAAR. Now, now, my dears, excuses must be made for youth. My little Lotte is a decent girl at heart. Go on, my son.

MAYOR. At the present time Herr Assistant Inspector of Buildings, Roads, and Mines Sperling is minded to bring into his home as his lawfully wedded wife my above mentioned daughter, Lotte.

HERR STAAR. All this we know well enough. Proceed.

MAYOR. It now appears that on the eve of the espousal in question another suitor nourishing equally Christian intentions declares himself.

ALL. Who? Who?

MAYOR. He who has been so very particularly recommended to me by his Excellency, the Prime Minister: to wit, Herr Olmers.

(*General exclamations*)

MAYOR. What does my good family think of this, after mature reflection?

FRAU STAAR. Well now—

HERR STAAR. It seems to me—

FRAU BRENDEL. As far as I am concerned—

FRAU MORGENROTH. I have my own thoughts—

FRAU BRENDEL. This marrying into Berlin is seldom a success. There are examples.

FRAU STAAR. Exactly, cousin: the daughter of the Administrative Secretary.

FRAU BRENDEL. Remember the hurrahs and the glory when she married that journalist?

FRAU MORGENROTH. Three new dresses all at once.

FRAU STAAR. Less than a year went by and back she came with a brat in her arms.

FRAU BRENDEL. And here she sits now, starving away.[5]

FRAU MORGENROTH. All the silk finery is sold.

FRAU STAAR. Naturally. How else can she make ends meet?

FRAU BRENDEL. What with prices rising every day.

FRAU MORGENROTH. How true; the last time my girl went marketing butter had gone up by yet another penny.

FRAU STAAR. What's the world coming to?

FRAU BRENDEL. In spite of which, never a day goes by but Frau Secretary to the Board of Management Wittman must be entertaining in her home.

FRAU MORGENROTH. Didn't I hear she had baked more fresh pastries yesterday?

[5] In the original, she gnaws at the *Hungertuch* (literally the hunger-cloth), namely, the veil covering the altar during Lent.

FRAU STAAR. You don't say!

FRAU BRENDEL. When you think that her husband has a mere part-time appointment.

FRAU STAAR. Where do people find the money?

FRAU MORGENROTH. As for that, if I wanted to talk—

FRAU STAAR and FRAU BRENDEL. Do, do, my dear.

MAYOR. Another time, with all due deference. Now, to return to my letter—

HERR STAAR. What can you be thinking of, brother? The man has no relations.

FRAU BRENDEL. One knows nothing of his birth.

FRAU MORGENROTH. Is he a Mister, a Sir, a Your Grace, or what?[6]

FRAU BRENDEL. As you know, since time immemorial all the *good* families of Piffelheim have intermarried.

FRAU MORGENROTH. Here we marry in order to be *connected*.

HERR STAAR. So everybody can be helpful to everybody in the municipal council.

FRAU BRENDEL (*to the Mayor*). You, dear cousin, know this better than anyone.

FRAU MORGENROTH. A stranger is like a fox in a cozy chicken coop.

HERR STAAR. The man knows nothing of our worthy old customs—

FRAU BRENDEL. Sneers at our respectable manners—

FRAU MORGENROTH. Poisons our precious young people who are bad enough and getting worse every day—

FRAU STARR. How true, cousin. When *we* were young—

FRAU MORGENROTH. How true, how true!

FRAU STAAR. But I wonder how you can forget the most important point! The man is nothing—not even an assistant to some clerk or something of the kind. I really like that! The daughter of a Mayor, also Senior Church Elder, the granddaughter of a Deputy Collector of the Revenue! Only the cream of the crop for him!

MAYOR. Thus the *conclusum* of our deliberation has been—

FRAU STAAR. She is not for him.

MAYOR. *Bene! Optime!* I concur. The question that remains is by what tactful means we should apprise him of our decision. The dutiful respect we owe to His Excellency the Minister makes it imperative that we proceed with every precaution.

FRAU STAAR. If we ask him to dine with us every day, he ought to be

---

[6] In the original, Frau Morgenroth wants to know whether, in writing to Olmers, one is to address him as *Hochedel* (highly noble) or *Wohledel* (roughly, quite noble). Neither of these rises as high as "Your Grace" does in English, but, as usual, the English translator has to make do with what is available. Kotzebue himself was normally addressed in formal letters as *Hochwohlgeborner Herr*, making him "highly well-born."

content.

MAYOR. This *is* something.

FRAU BRENDEL. You might offer him a toast on behalf of the Town Council
of Piffelheim.

MAYOR. That, on the other hand, is excessive.

FRAU MORGENROTH. He could be godfather at the next family baptism.

MAYOR. Possibly.

HERR STAAR. How about—since what really matters to him is to settle down
in Piffelheim—how about suggesting he take another wife?

MAYOR. Now *that* strikes me as a useful idea.

FRAU STAAR. Very good; but who?

HERR STAAR (*to the Mayor*). Your Ursula. She is eight, going on nine. He
can wait, take time to acquire a respectable position with the help of His
Excellency; manners, by living among us; and an education through my
circulating library; and finally ask for her hand again.

FRAU STAAR. I'm for that. When the time comes we can still decide one way
or the other.

MAYOR. But suppose he doesn't want to wait that long. I know these young
gentlemen. Once they get the itch to be married, they're off like wild
horses.

HERR STAAR. Well, I'm also willing to offer him a riper beauty.

ALL. Who? Who?

HERR STAAR. Here, our own cousin, our widow of the Timber and Fishery
Administrator.

FRAU BRENDEL (*blushing*). You're joking. . . .

HERR STAAR. She is eight months into her widowhood.

FRAU BRENDEL. Almost nine months, Herr Vice-Churchwarden, almost nine
months.

HERR STAAR. She has means. She can buy him a title—they're not expen-
sive. And of course, he *is* a pretty fellow.

FRAU BRENDEL. Yes, he's a pretty fellow—no one can deny it.

HERR STAAR. And in that way too he would come into the family.

FRAU STAAR. Which seems to be the point uppermost in his mind.

MAYOR. Well, cousin, what do you say?

FRAU BRENDEL (*hiding behind her fan*). Oh dear, let the good Lord decide.

[10] (*Enter Olmers*)

OLMERS. Forgive a lover's impatience which drives me restlessly hither and
fro. I see you together here. Perhaps my fate has been decided. May I
entertain the flattering hope that I shall soon be admitted to this circle?

MAYOR (*embarrassed and ceremonious*). Yes—no doubt—His Excellency,
the Herr Minister, has been so urgent in his recommendation—even if certain wishes cannot be precisely—

FRAU STAAR. Satisfaction might be found—

HERR STAAR. By way of certain modifications—

FRAU BRENDEL. Please don't go on!

FRAU MORGENROTH. Thank heaven, our family is a large one—

FRAU BRENDEL. I'm all blushes.

OLMERS. How am I to interpret these broken sentences? Kindly make yourself clear, Herr Mayor.

MAYOR. My mother is the head of the family. I yield the floor to her. (*Exits*)

OLMERS. Well, then, Madam, I await the decision from your lips. (*Frau Staar sneezes*)

ALL except OLMERS. God bless you.

FRAU STAAR (*aside*). The barbarian doesn't even say God bless you. (*Aloud*) No, Herr Olmers, *Madam* has nothing to say. (*To Herr Staar*) You may speak for me, my son, you are acquainted with my thoughts. (*Exits*)

OLMERS. Quickly, sir, relieve me of a tormenting uncertainty.

HERR STAAR. A delicate affair. Threading needles and stitching couples together is women's business. I beg you, therefore, to turn to these ladies. (*Exits*)

OLMERS. Well, ladies?

FRAU MORGENROTH. A young man's heart, my dear sir, does not always know what it really desires. Often it wanders far from the goal, unaware that Amor is about to bless it through a happy exchange.

OLMERS. What is that supposed to mean?

FRAU MORGENROTH. Ask my cousin. (*Exits*)

OLMERS. Will *you* finally solve this riddle for me?

FRAU BRENDEL (*simpering*). The family has certain intentions—it feels that a compensation is due—propositions are being made—projects elaborated—but you must be sensible that a young woman cannot, in all modesty, be drawn into heaven knows what after but ten months of widow-hood. (*Exits*)

OLMERS (*alone*). What the devil am I to make of this? Living in a capital all one's life can lead to plenty of trouble, I see. A fellow happens to land in a small town, and then stands in it like an owl on a pole with the crows flapping their wings at him, mad at seeing a stranger.   [11]

(*Enter Lotte*)   [12]

LOTTE. Are you alone at last?

OLMERS. I am, but not in the best of spirits.

LOTTE. I've a thousand things to tell you.

OLMERS. And I only one.

LOTTE. That you love me? Is that the one?

OLMERS. Exactly.

LOTTE. There's no time for that now. That abominable Sperling is trailing me like a bloodhound. Oh God, here he is again.

[13] (*Enter Sperling*)

OLMERS (*softly*). Shall I throw him out the door?

LOTTE (*softly*). For heaven's sake, don't go spoiling everything.

SPERLING. Here I am, here I am, my lovely Lottchen, as true and close to you
    as the train of your dress.

OLMERS. If so, you're in danger of being trod upon.

SPERLING.

>   The cruel maiden trod, alas
>   Upon the violet in the grass—[7]

OLMERS. Wicked maiden!

SPERLING. Fiddle-faddle. Right, my sweetie? *We* know where we stand.

OLMERS. Not before the altar at any rate.

SPERLING. Soon! Soon!

>   A crown of myrtles in her golden hair,
>   To the altar walks the happy pair.

OLMERS (*getting very irritated*). Suppose, however, Herr Assistant Inspector
    of Buildings, Roads, and Mines, that first there must occur a little breaking
    of necks between you and a rival?

SPERLING. What? What?

OLMERS (*coming closer to him*). Suppose one told you in plain, one-syllable
    words—

SPERLING (*irritated*). Well, what?

LOTTE (*stepping between them*). You're so right, Herr Olmers, it *would* be
    best to ask Herr Sperling's advice.

SPERLING. What about?

LOTTE (*winking at Olmers*). Trust me, Herr Sperling is an expert.

SPERLING. What in, my angel?

LOTTE (*to Sperling*). You see, this gentleman is trying to finish a novel he has
    been writing.

OLMERS. I'm writing a novel?

LOTTE (*aside to him*). Silence!

SPERLING. About knights in armor?

LOTTE. You might say there's a knight in it. And, in order to bring about the
    violent end, he simply *must* contrive a secret interview between the knight
    and his beloved.

OLMERS. Yes, I simply must.

SPERLING. Oh, I understand.

LOTTE. Unfortunately, the poor girl is being watched from morning to night.
    Now it's the father, now it's the mother, now the rival—

SPERLING. Aha! There's a rival in the picture, eh? Some repulsive clown, I

---

[7] Sperling is quoting from Goethe's famous lyric, *Das Veilchen* (The Violet). The couplet below
seems to be Sperling's very own.

imagine.

OLMERS. Exactly, my dear sir: an unbearable fool.

SPERLING (*laughing*). I see.

LOTTE. And so, a trick has to be devised in order to give the girl an opportunity of speaking in secret with her knight because (*meaningfully*) she has things of extreme importance to tell him.

SPERLING. Which the rival mustn't overhear?

LOTTE. Of course not.

SPERLING. I understand. And Herr Olmers is at a loss how to bring it off.

OLMERS. I am. If you were good enough to come to my help with some useful advice—

SPERLING. With all my heart. Nothing is easier. Let me see. . . . Well, now, for instance, a daylight interview is out of the question, because this clod of a rival never leaves her side.

OLMERS. Precisely.

SPERLING. Therefore by night. Namely at the witching hour—midnight.

LOTTE. *That* is a little ticklish, because, although the girl is pert and spritely, she is also portrayed as a model of virtue.

OLMERS. This doesn't look to me like an insuperable obstacle inasmuch as the knight is already more or less her fiancé.

LOTTE. No, Herr Olmers, your heroine's honor is too close to my heart. Midnight is out. An evening tryst—maybe.

SPERLING. Evening is perfect. I suppose the rival is a sleepyhead who goes to bed early.

LOTTE. Right.

SPERLING. So then: evening it is. They meet in a long, out of the way corridor in the castle, dimly lit by a flickering light—

LOTTE. Oh no! The place is already thoroughly described, and has no such corridor.

SPERLING. Or else a garden where, between the darksome yews—

LOTTE. You forget, Herr Sperling, that our virtuous maiden does not frequent darksome yews.

OLMERS. Still, my feeling is that we *could* allow her to go into the garden.

LOTTE. No, we can't; the garden doesn't suit her.

SPERLING. In that case, why not let the knight take the bull by the horns and just slip into her bedroom?

LOTTE. God forbid! The bedroom suits her even less.

OLMERS. It almost looks as if she didn't trust her sweetheart.

LOTTE. She does. But our critics demand the strictest morality. No, gentlemen, the girl won't be talked into anything of the sort.

SPERLING. Well, we're in trouble. God knows I'd like to be of use to you, but I'm afraid, Herr Olmers, you've painted the girl's character almost a little too austere, too virtuous.

OLMERS. You're quite right. I can see that in the end she will have to marry the silly rival.

SPERLING. No, no, no! That musn't happen. I forbid it. Let's see how we can prevent it. What about. . . . Well, now, the only thing the girl might consent to is a brief meeting by the entrance-door to the house before bed time. Everybody would still be awake—people passing to and fro, the night watchman, and so forth. What do you think?

OLMERS. A wonderful idea.

LOTTE. It's not *quite* as irreproachable as I might wish—

SPERLING. Don't worry; I assume the entire responsibility. (*To Olmers*) Contrive the meeting as I said; no one can possibly object.

LOTTE. Well, Herr Olmers, if you like the plan—

OLMERS (*to Sperling*). I'll follow your advice with the greatest pleasure.

SPERLING (*rubbing his hands contentedly*). So now we've helped the poor respectable girl out of her trouble.

LOTTE (*making a curtsy*). And she has you to thank for it.

SPERLING. The pleasure's all mine. What if we arranged the scene so that on top of everything we made an ass of the rival?

LOTTE. Yes, let's.

SPERLING. Is he dumb enough to be duped, Herr Olmers?

OLMERS. Oh, I can vouch for that!

LOTTE. What if the girl arranged the rendez-vous with her lover in the rival's very presence?

SPERLING. Bravo! That *would* be an amusing scene.

LOTTE. We could even get him to laugh at the trick himself!

SPERLING (*laughing*). Better and better.

LOTTE. Listen! The party's breaking up. Good night, gentlemen. Perhaps we'll laugh even more heartily tomorrow, because I suppose by then Herr Olmers will have done what's needed.

OLMERS. You may count on it.

LOTTE. Well, then, *au revoir*. (*Exits*)

SPERLING. You're buckling down to work today still?

OLMERS. Yes; one has to catch the spark, you know.

SPERLING. You're so right. Look here—when your novel is done—could I ask you for a copy?

OLMERS. It will be dedicated to you. (*Exits*)

[14] SPERLING (*alone*). Too much honor, sir. Far too much honor. Is our Herr Novelist twitting me? I could almost believe it.

> He puffs himself like a department chief;[8]
> Hopes for gold and fame; God grant him luck!

---

[8] Literally a "superintendent"—according to Guignard a high church dignitary.

Watch out! I'll see his novel come to grief
When twenty critics drag it through the muck.
And yet without my help where would he be?
Walking like a crab, backward to the sea.
That lovers' meeting: 'Twas I that prompted it:
He had it from my talent and my wit.

ACT 4

The street in front of the Mayor's house, with the latter standing stage right or left and his brother's on the other side of the street. Under the roof of Herr Staar's house is Sperling's garret, while before it stands an unlit lamp post, though night has fallen. Instead, several lights are still burning in the upper stories of both houses. NOTE. The two houses are so angled that the spectators can fully see anyone leaning out of a window. The lamp post can be placed somewhat upstage.[1]

[1] OLMERS (*alone, coming out of the Mayor's house*). Thank God, at any rate, that people go to bed early in small towns. I haven't had a minute to myself all day. Nothing but questions, compliments, endless chatter. They're as inquisitive as can be and yet they always know it all. Their precious guest can't be left alone for a second; wherever I turn they're after me. I must eat though I'm not hungry, drink though I'm not thirsty, sit down though not tired; gawk at their wonderful sights, listen to their small-town gossip, and praise and admire all day long. I'd gladly endure it all to possess my darling—but fortune isn't smiling yet—I've not even had a few words alone with her to sweeten this wearisome trial. She promised to meet me here as soon as all was quiet in the house. Will she keep her word?

[2] (*Enter Lotte; she slips out of the house and taps Olmers on the shoulder*)
LOTTE. Yes, my doubting Thomas, she does keep her word.
OLMERS. At last, my darling, at last we're by ourselves! And now I can pour my heart out again[2] —
LOTTE. Why? I already know everything you want to tell me.
OLMERS. But I must seize the precious moments—
LOTTE. You're all alike. The lover complains he hasn't enough time to repeat

---

[1] The classical filiation of the stage set here is striking, leading us, through Molière (for instance) straight back to Terence. "The scene [in Terence], always the same, represents immutably a little square or a street in Athens upon which give the houses of the principal personages. . . . At the center of the stage there must have been an altar, serving as an ideal hiding-place for the characters who wanted to listen without being seen." (M. Scandola: *Publio Terenzio Afro: Tutte le commedie,* Milano 1951, pp. 9-10). Here the altar has turned into a lamppost: one flame yields to another.

[2] Schumacher criticizes this scene because it has no plot-value; that is to say, the lovers "pour their hearts out" yet do nothing, though classical comedy all but demands that at this point they should devise a clever contrivance. Instead, the trick-motif seems to have exhausted itself in Act Three, in resolving the minor problem of "how to meet alone" rather than the major one, "how to get married." But Kotzebue sets up an alternative which seems to me satisfactory enough. The longing to be by themselves for awhile after several months of separation is perfectly natural. What happens in consequence of this natural but plotless tryst is (as will be seen) that the decisive opportunity will fall into the lovers' laps.

a thousand times what he's already said a thousand times. The husband, on the other hand, who could hold forth from morning to night, spends the day muttering and grumbling.

OLMERS. I hope you don't believe—

LOTTE. That you will do so too? I'd love not to believe it. But truth is truth: lovers and larks sing in springtime. Come fall, a girl has to be grateful if they haven't flown off altogether.

OLMERS. I swear to you—

LOTTE. Don't swear too loud. We're surrounded by a couple of dozen ears. Over there is my father's bedroom: his light is still on. And there's my grandmother's; I imagine she's still singing an evening hymn. Across the street lives my uncle, still leafing through his novels. And in the attic I can fancy Herr Sperling composing another sonnet to myself. Before long the night watchman will come tooting his horn and the fire-watch will appear with his rattle.[3]

OLMERS. Charming. I suppose the street lighter is about due as well to light this lamp.

LOTTE. No. There we're safe. The moon is shining tonight.

OLMERS. Only before dawn!

LOTTE. It doesn't matter. When the almanac says Moon we wisely economize.

OLMERS. As for coping with those wonderful paving-stones—

LOTTE. Don't be snippy, and thank your stars you came away with a mere bruise on your nose.

OLMERS. But dearest, wouldn't we have been far more comfortable and undisturbed in my room?

LOTTE. Do you think so? Yes, you do. A pity that it's not a Piffelheim custom for young girls to visit sweethearts in their rooms. Here in the street, I am, in a manner of speaking, protected by all my relatives.

OLMERS. And could even, if need be, call the night watchman for help.

LOTTE. Yes, Herr Olmers, I could.

OLMERS. I shouldn't have thought that, as my bride—

LOTTE. I am not your bride yet. And if you continue to play the fool, I doubt whether I shall ever be.

OLMERS. Play the fool? In what way?

LOTTE. What Satan prompted you to call my grandmother Frau Staar? She is Frau Deputy Collector of the Revenue and don't you ever forget it.

OLMERS. Excellent. Tomorrow she'll have her title bestowed at least three hundred times.

LOTTE. The more, the better. And why didn't you eat your dinner this

---

[3] A rattle, revolving noisily around its handle, was used throughout Europe by fire-watchmen and night-watchmen alike.

evening?

OLMERS. Because I was full.

LOTTE. What of it? What sort of lover is it who won't brave an indigestion for his mistress?

OLMERS. So be it. I'll eat like another Jack Pudding.[4]

LOTTE. And why did you keep yawning while my father was telling you all about that endless lawsuit?

OLMERS. Precisely because it was endless.

LOTTE. Too bad. I enjoin you to listen with rapt attention.

OLMERS. To a lawsuit, when you are sitting across the table?

LOTTE. My sitting across from you didn't keep you from yawning like an alderman. And when my uncle began to boast of his circulating library, were you or weren't you crazy to say it was all rubbish?

OLMERS. Yes—nothing but rubbish—those robbers and bandits, this sentimental versifying, these pious almanacs. . . .

LOTTE. What concern is that of yours? We believe in our good taste. We look down on gross human nature.[5]

OLMERS. Fine. Tomorrow I'll sing the praises of all the Romantic geniuses louder than they do themselves.

LOTTE. It will be hard, but do try.

OLMERS. To win you I'll face any hardship.

LOTTE. With all this you'll still fall short of the goal. The thing most needful is still missing.

OLMERS. Namely?

LOTTE. A title, my friend, a title! Without title, Piffelheim is closed to you. For us, a bit of parchment with a seal on it is worth more than gold in your pocket. A title is the handle by which we grasp a fellow creature. Without it we don't know where to get hold of him. Here no one asks, "Is he

---

[4] Kotzebue has, "Good. I'll eat like the famous Paul Butterbrot." Guignard explains Paul Buttered-Bread as a character of popular comedy, similar to the *really* famous Hanswurst and Pickelherring. My guess is that Paul Butterbrot was the invention of an ephemerally applauded clown of the day. All these Jack Pudding personages are indefatigable gluttons.

[5] Speaking for Kotzebue, Lotte adds, "We don't read Wieland and Engel anymore." Olmers then replies that he will make sure to praise the *Kraftgenies* of the day; that is to say, the "powerful geniuses" of Romanticism, and heirs of the *Sturm und Drang* writers for whom individual and unlicensed "genius" was the ideal. In a loose adaptation, Olmers might be given the line, "I shall praise the titanic geniuses of the day." As for the two writers Lotte names, posterity has sharply separated them. C. M. Wieland (1733-1813), whose reputation was indeed in decline at the time, remains, for us, a standard German author and a fair representative of the pre-Romantic spirit. J. J. Engel (1741-1802), instead, is remembered only as the director of the National Theater in Berlin, inaugurated in 1786. His novels and plays are forgotten. But Kotzebue had good reason to like him. As a boy in Weimar he had been moved by Engel's maudlin *The Grateful Son*. In Reval, between 1784 and 1788, he had produced several of Engel's plays. But most important, Engel's acceptance and production of *Menschenhass und Reue* at the National Theater in 1789 had sped Kotzebue off on his astonishing parabola of fame. As Engel died on June 28, 1802, it is not certain that he saw the little compliment by his admired friend before shuffling off his mortal coil.

learned, is he wealthy?" The question is, "What title has he got?" If you haven't twelve to fifteen syllables in front of your name, don't meddle into the conversation, though you may know ten times as much as anyone else. We take our titles to bed and to the grave—indeed we entertain a secret hope that on Judgment Day the last trump will call us out by some new little titles. In short, my handsome friend, you do not get me without a title. My grandmother will not have it that on the day the banns are solemnly published, all that the minister can say is "The groom is Herr Karl Olmers."

OLMERS. What if I told you that I *have* secured a fine little title?

LOTTE. You have? Then our troubles are over. But why didn't you say so at once?[6]

OLMERS. I didn't know—

LOTTE. You should have known. Why, do you think only Piffelheim is infected by this title-pest? Believe me, it's everywhere the same.[7] Hush! I hear a noise. It's Sperling's window. Don't tell me he was spying on us.

(*Sperling appears at the window*)   [3]

SPERLING (*declaiming*).

  Your lover knocks at dead of night!
  Sweetheart, do you wake or sleep?
  How fares the love that burned so bright?
  Are you consoled? Or do you weep?[8]

LOTTE (*low*). I take it he's haranguing me.

SPERLING. Over there are the dear little windows behind which my charmer dwells. All dim and dark. Perhaps those sweet victorious eyes have closed by now.

LOTTE. Do you hear this, sir? Victorious!

OLMERS. He's telling me nothing I didn't know.

[6] Why indeed didn't he say so at once? Guignard notes the "deliberate improbability" and Schumacher lucidly remarks that Kotzebue has artificially kept this revelation from the other characters so as not to abort the play, since, had Olmers presented himself earlier with his title, Sperling would undoubtedly have been sent on his way and the play would have been over. But is Kotzebue really cheating? It can be argued that in keeping his title to himself, Olmers has been illustrating the very *savoir-faire* he and Lotte uphold—the good manners of the Residenz. As a true gentleman—though a bit light-headed and a mite on the impudent side (an image of Kotzebue himself?)—he would have considered it vulgar and Piffelheimish to parade his "addition." Seen in this light, his reticence appears psychologically probable and thematically significant. But a subtler defence would take yet another approach, to wit, that Kotzebue, master of his craft, can afford to toy with the motif of Olmers's title—can afford to bestow it or withhold it from him—*because he does not need it* to wind up his plot. The seemingly vital revelation is in fact a structural extra, a luxury. But this will be pursued in note 20.

[7] In French in the original: "C'est partout comme chez nous."

[8] Sperling is reciting a half stanza from G. A. Bürger's famous ballad "Lenore" (1774). Kotzebue's audience would immediately have recognized the lines. A few spectators might have been amused by Sperling's grand delusion, since the heroine of Bürger's poem was in love with her betrothed to the point of deliriously blaspheming against God.

SPERLING. Let tender melodies beguile the pure maiden's slumber. (*He tunes a fiddle*)

LOTTE. Merciful gods! A serenade! The man will scratch the whole neighborhood awake.

OLMERS. Devil take him!

SPERLING (*plays and sings*).

Tralduralduraldural o hear,

traldural the lyre plays—

LOTTE. And here comes the night watchman. That's all we needed. Hurry—behind the lamp post. (*They hide as best they can*)

[4]   (*Enter the night watchman blowing on his horn*)

WATCHMAN. Nine o'clock and all's well.

SPERLING. You rogue! You're interrupting my music.

WATCHMAN. What's that to me? If the gentleman wishes to sing out the hours himself, he's welcome to come down. (*Singing*) Nine o'clock and all's well.

SPERLING (*playing and singing at the same time*).

Dalduralduraldural

Oh here I am—

[5]   (*Frau Staar appears at her window singing*)

FRAU STAAR. Now the woods[9] —

(*calls out*). God in heaven! Such noise! (*Sings*) Now the woods are resting.

WATCHMAN (*at the same time*). Nine o'clock at the tower!

SPERLING (*at the same time*). Your faithful lover stands before you, sweet.

WATCHMAN. All right, all right—I'm done. (*Exit*)

[6]   (*Herr Staar appears at the window*)

HERR STAAR. Neighbor Sperling, stop your bawling, will you? You're beginning to fret the beasts in the stable.

FRAU STAAR. And deserving people at their evening prayers.

SPERLING. I just wanted to serenade my bride.

FRAU STAAR. Come now. She's long asleep. (*She shuts the window, resuming her evensong*)

HERR STAAR. This has been a wild day. Why, it's nearly ten o'clock!

SPERLING. And who's to blame? That adventurer from Berlin.

LOTTE (*to Olmers*). Namely you.

HERR STAAR. And our Mistress Impertinence whose eyes usually fall shut by eight o'clock.

OLMERS (*to Lotte*). So much for you.

SPERLING. I almost had the impression she never took her eyes off that

---

[9] Like Frau Morgenroth in I, 13, Frau Staar is singing a hymn composed by Paul Gerhardt (1607-76).

LOTTE (*to Olmers*). He means you.

HERR STAAR. The worse for her! We give ourselves modest airs—

OLMERS. Meaning you.

SPERLING. But we're willing to put up with a stranger's cheek.

LOTTE (*to Olmers*). Meaning you.

HERR STAAR. My niece thinks she can do anything she likes because of her pretty little face.

OLMERS. Remember that.

SPERLING. And Herr Olmers because of his high-flown philosophizing.

LOTTE. Kindly take note.

HERR STAAR. Well, tomorrow it's all coming to an end.

LOTTE. God willing.

SPERLING. Tomorrow we celebrate the betrothal.

OLMERS. Between you and me.

FRAU STAAR. Sleep well, Herr Assistant Inspector of Buildings, Roads, and Mines.

SPERLING. Sweet dreams, Herr Vice-Churchwarden. (*Exeunt*)

OLMERS. Gone at last! [7]

LOTTE. But now it's our turn to go in.

OLMERS. Why? It's such a beautiful, mild evening. Let's take a walk to the city gate.

LOTTE. Are you mad? Why not all the way to the quarry?

OLMERS. Well then, up and down the street a bit.

LOTTE. Nor that either. This shows you what chances a girl takes once she departs an inch from the strait and narrow. Because I allowed the gentleman to lure me to the door, he quite believes he can go wandering the wide world with me.

OLMERS. A harmless walk—

LOTTE. A joyous walk through life hand in hand with you. But no such walk before the wedding. And so good night. Tomorrow at sun-up step forward with your title and give punctilious heed to all my other commands.[10]

OLMERS. Good night, splendid girl! But you won't deny me a kiss?

LOTTE. A handshake is already too much. Oh God! Here's a lantern rushing towards us! It's that wall-eyed bailiff, I think. Let's hide again! Hurry! (*They step again behind the lamp post*)

(*Enter Klaus with his lantern*) [8]

KLAUS (*out of breath*). Uff! I'm destroyed, done for, dead—and maybe even dismissed, alas alas alas! But what's the use? The Mayor must be told— told tonight—so he can sound the alarm. (*He knocks at the Mayor's door*)

---

[10] Lotte is in revolt against provincial life and manners, but not against middle-class standards of maidenly behavior. Olmers, instead, is allowed as much rakishness as could be entertained on a German stage in 1802.

Hey—holla—hey!

MAYOR (*inside*). Who's knocking this late at night?

KLAUS. Open up! The nation is in danger.

MAYOR (*upstairs at the window*). Klaus! Is that you? What do you want?

KLAUS. Oh, Your Worship, I'm a dead man.

MAYOR. What's happened?

KLAUS. That woman—our delinquent—

MAYOR. Well?

KLAUS. Gone to the devil.

MAYOR. What?

KLAUS. Flown the coop!

MAYOR. God forbid!

KLAUS. My honor! My reputation! My bonus![11] I'll drown myself in the pond!

MAYOR. Hush up, will you! This business must be grappled with in silence. Wait for me. I'm coming down. (*He closes the window*)

KLAUS. Miserable wretch that I am! Who is going to stand in the pillory tomorrow? There's not a Christian in this town who will help me in my hour of need.

[9]   (*Enter the Mayor in his brocaded robe*)

MAYOR. All right, Klaus, let me have a detailed report concerning this catastrophe.

KLAUS. Your Worship is aware that it's my duty to bring the delinquent half a pound of bread every evening and a pitcher of water from the city's moat. Well, I did it tonight. I found her cheerful, in high spirits, and snug in her manacles. Her good bed made of soft old straw had been given a thorough shake. So then, I wish her good luck for the honor that's awaiting her tomorrow, shut the door, lock it, and go to bed. An hour later my wife prods my ribs with her sharp elbow and says, "Listen up there how those cats are miaowing." "What cats?" says I suspiciously. "They've been forbidden to show their faces at City Hall ever since one of them committed the indecency of having her kittens on the Herr Mayor's chair."

MAYOR. Go on.

KLAUS. I prick up my ears—I listen—I make conjectures—I register surprise—all of which may have taken about half an hour.

MAYOR. Much too long!

KLAUS. At last I gather my wits together. I rise from bed, light my lantern, tiptoe upstairs, unlock, stick in my head—thunder strike me! The nest is empty—the bird has taken wing.

MAYOR. With Satan's help?

---

[11] *Sporteln* in the original: a fee, a perquisite; probably the extra money Klaus got for watching over the delinquent—who, it will be noted, is imprisoned in the town hall itself.

KLAUS. How else? She'd stripped off her handcuffs, broken through the wall, climbed up to my pantry, and made off with a ham and three sausages!

MAYOR. A witch! She must be burned alive. I'll make a report to the King's Bench! The Chief Forester shall deliver the royal kindling for the stake.[12]

KLAUS. First though, I wish we could catch her.

MAYOR. Damnable trick. Nine years long I have allowed this affair to darken my existence; the paperwork is piled up to the ceiling; (*pathetically*) tomorrow at long last I was going to reap the fruit of my efforts—all Piffelheim awaits the festive hour—the pillory beckons, ready to honor the city's highest magistrates—and lo! my proud expectations have burst like the soap bubbles of our street urchins!

KLAUS. My reputation! My bonus! My ham!

MAYOR. Did you find no trace of some infamous hand that may have expedited her escape?

KLAUS. Not a Christian soul except Satan. The woman was a camp follower in the war against the French[13] —that's where she became friends with the devil. And cunning besides! She knew how to string words together like a duchess and did nothing but read all day. She even left a couple of books on the table along with a dirty scrap of paper. Myself, I can't read.

MAYOR. Give me that note! (*He reads by the lantern's light*) "The honorable Council will forgive me if I spoil tomorrow's entertainment"— Entertainment? We were dead serious!

KLAUS. If we could lay hands on you again—we'd show you entertainment!

MAYOR (*reading*). "The time finally grew heavy on my hands. I felt like breathing fresh air"—Couldn't she have waited until she stood in the pillory?

KLAUS. The woman's ingratitude! Nine years we fed her.

MAYOR (*reading*). "I owe my liberation to the Herr Vice-Churchwarden." What? What's that? To my brother? Has he gone mad?

KLAUS. Thank the Lord we have *him* to blame.

MAYOR (*reading*). "Who was kind enough to lend me a number of lovely books out of his circulating library." The devil gave him *that* idea! (*Reading*)—"Among them Baron von der Trenck's *Memoirs of My Several Escapes from Prison*"[14] —I wish he were sitting in one himself! (*Reading*)

---

[12] The last known witch-burning in the German world took place in Posen in 1793. A witch had been burned in Glarus (Switzerland) in 1782, another in Kempten in 1775; and as late as 1813 an arsonist and his female accomplice were burned alive in Berlin. Thus in a serious play this passage would have looked less preposterous than might be supposed.

[13] Literally, a sutler (provisioner) in Lorraine. Klaus is referring to the War of the First Coalition against the French, from which Prussia prudently withdrew in 1795.

[14] Frederick von Trenck, rogue and writer, guillotined by the French in 1794, published his *Memoirs* in 1787; they became immediate best-sellers and were read and reprinted for a long time in and out of Germany. An English translation appeared almost at once. Numerous other English editions followed under a variety of titles, e.g., *The Life, Adventures and Uncommon Escapes of Frederick, baron Trenck.* The title in my text is made up from these variants.

"This book taught me the courage, patience, and skill to contrive my escape. The moment has come—I am about to flee—"

KLAUS. Not true; she's fled already.

MAYOR (*reading*). "I thank His Worship the Herr Mayor for his mouldy bread."—What rubbish! Did she expect cake? (*Reading*) "And Herr Bailiff Klaus for his slimy water."

KLAUS. It's a lie! Our moat has underground springs.

MAYOR (*reading*). "My fondest remembrance to all the citizens of Piffelheim. I am heartily sorry to have stolen that cow nine years ago, as she was nothing but skin and bones."

KLAUS. That much is correct.

MAYOR (*reading*). "May Heaven therefore bless the Herr Mayor with abundance of fat, and may he also enjoy tomorrow's public banquet. Eve Schnurrwinkel." A curse on this Eve!

KLAUS. You serpent!

MAYOR. You basilisk! Won't the Rummelsburger be happy now! My honor! The name of Piffelheim! All blasted! Listen, Klaus! Can't you think of some loyal citizen who'd agree—you know—for patriotic reasons—for the honor of the thing—we could put a disguise on him—

KLAUS. Nobody will do it, Your Worship. They're all willing to be spectators; but the moment they're asked to step forward for the good of the country, why, suddenly nobody's home.

MAYOR. Woe is me!—and—my brother! My damned brother, sleeping like a baby![15] (*He drums at his brother's house*) Wake up, wake up, wake up!

HERR STAAR (*upstairs at the window*). What the devil—Who's knocking this late? Get away from here! I don't sell coffee after ten o'clock. (*He bangs the window shut*)

MAYOR. What do you say to that jackass? I, the Mayor, also Senior Church Elder, coming to the grocer to buy coffee! (*He knocks again*) Hey there! Holla!

HERR STAAR (*at the window*). If you're not gone this instant, I'll wake up the watch!

MAYOR. Herr brother, you can be happy that the watch is asleep as usual.

HERR STAAR. Is that really you, brother? Why up so late?

MAYOR. Bad news. Come down and I'll tell you.

HERR STAAR. There's no fire, I hope.

MAYOR. I wish to God half the town were burning, and your house the first to go.

HERR STAAR. God forbid! I'm coming down. (*He shuts the window*)

---

[15] Kotzebue has "sleeping *quasi re bene gesta*"—"as though all were for the best." In 1802, one could still satirize a man for using Latin. In this respect, the Mayor derives from a long tradition of comic pedants spouting Latin at their helpless listeners.

MAYOR. Yes, come down. A body of worthy citizens is rejoicing at the coming of daylight; they have bespoke fresh vestments and slaughtered the fattest pigs. When they hear it's all over and done with they're apt to storm his house and nail his whole library to the pillory.

KLAUS. So much the better. Nothing but riffraff robbers in these books.

(*Enter Herr Staar in nightdress*) [10]

HERR STAAR. Well, what has happened?

MAYOR. You can be proud of what you've accomplished. You deserve a prize.

HERR STAAR. Who? Me?

MAYOR. You and your damned books.

HERR STAAR. Damned? I'll have you know they've all been approved by the censor.

MAYOR. Who gave you the authority to help a delinquent while her time away?

HERR STAAR. Good grief! Everybody wants to read nowadays, and jail-birds get as bored as aristocrats. Now and then—out of compassion—I slipped her some bandit or human monster.

MAYOR. Wonderful.

HERR STAAR. But also a collection of hymns, and these gave her spirits a mighty lift.[16]

MAYOR. Splendid! They lifted her straight to the devil.

HERR STAAR. What's that?

MAYOR. She broke through the wall.

KLAUS. She stole my ham.

MAYOR. And kindly thanks you, my dear brother.

HERR STAAR. Thanks me?

MAYOR. Here, take the light, and read.

SPERLING (*at the window*). Whence this murmuring, this whispering, this buzzing and this humming?

MAYOR. There we have it. All the fools of Piffelheim are about to wake up.

SPERLING. What do I see, hear, and guess?

MAYOR. If Herr Sperling is nimble on his feet, let him come down and go after her.

SPERLING. Did my fiancé run away? I descend on the wings of a stormy wind. (*He shuts the window*)

MAYOR (*to Herr Staar*). Well, how do you like the taste of it?

HERR STAAR. Brother, you can see I'm so astonished—

MAYOR. And how is that going to help me? I can't nail your astonishment to

---

[16] Kotzebue has Herr Staar giving Eva "a new spiritual song after Jakob Böhm"—the mystic (1575-1624) whose writings influenced a great deal of German religious verse. A touch here and there gives us a sense of Kotzebue's Voltairean irreverence towards orthodox and popular Christianity.

the pillory, can I?

[11] (*Enter Sperling in night dress*)

SPERLING. Here I am! Here I am! Who abducted her?

MAYOR. Satan.

SPERLING. I hear, I know, I understand; Satan's name is Olmers.

MAYOR. Nonsense! Who's talking about my daughter? The prisoner has escaped.

SPERLING. The prisoner?

KLAUS. In company with a ham and sausages.

MAYOR. My brother helped her break out.

HERR STAAR. She read Trenck's *Memoirs*.

SPERLING. Ye gods in heaven! What do I hear? What is dawning on me? No celebration tomorrow. No pillory. No betrothal. What's to become of my creations? I composed a sonnet on Mistress Schnurrwinkel and a triolet[17] on our three-legged gallows.

MAYOR. I wish the whole lot of you were hanging from it.

HERR STAAR. What's to be done?

MAYOR. We're standing here gaping like fools.[18]

SPERLING. And the solemn feast interrupted![19]

HERR STAAR. The Rummelsburger are going to laugh their heads off.

MAYOR. That's the least of it. What will they say in Berlin?

HERR STAAR. They'll talk about misrule.

MAYOR. Lack of foresight; negligence . . .

HERR STAAR. The Minister will be furious.

MAYOR. The King will have a fit.

HERR STAAR. You, brother, will be deposed.

MAYOR. And you, brother, will go to jail.

HERR STAAR. Woe is me!

MAYOR. Triple woe!

HERR STAAR. Ring the church-bells! After her!

MAYOR. At night, in the dark?

HERR STAAR. Have the street lamps lit at once!

MAYOR. We can't—the almanac says moonshine tonight.

HERR STAAR. Never mind. The welfare of the nation is at stake. I'll pay for the oil. Herr Klaus, here, right in front of my house. Start here.

KLAUS. Gladly, if it'll help me catch sight of my ham. (*As he sets about lighting the lamp his eyes fall on Lotte and Olmers*) Ha! The prisoner!

[17] A. W. Schlegel's grand satire against Kotzebue, *Honor Portal and Triumphal Arch for the Theater-President Kotzebue* (see the introductory essay), contained, among other morsels, a series of sonnets. Schlegel and other Romantics also favored medieval forms like the triolet.

[18] Literally, "like a herd of oxen on the mountain."

[19] Literally, "Such an interrupted sacrificial feast!"—an allusion, according to Guignard, to an opera bearing this title by a certain Peter von Winter (1754-1825).

(*Uproar*) And Satan next to her!

MAYOR. Stand forth, accursed creature.

KLAUS (*catching Lotte's arm*). Where are my sausages?

LOTTE (*kneeling*). Oh my father!

MAYOR and HERR STAAR. What's that? Lotte?

SPERLING. My bride!

KLAUS. Satan is playing a trick on us.

OLMERS (*coming forward*). Herr Mayor—

MAYOR and HERR STAAR. And our guest!

SPERLING. Didn't I tell you?

MAYOR. How did you get here, you hussy? What, sir, brings you to this place?

LOTTE. Tomorrow, father, tomorrow you'll be told everything there is to know. We were surprised by accident. I love Olmers. I detest Sperling.

SPERLING. Oh barbarous girl!

LOTTE. Olmers is well-to-do. He has a title. He went to school with the Minister and is his friend—

OLMERS. And as such, I should be delighted to intervene at court with regard to the embarrassing event to which I have just now been a witness. For it cannot be denied that it's a serious, indeed a critical matter.[20]

MAYOR (*trembling*). Do you mean it?

HERR STAAR. What can we expect?

OLMERS. You, Herr Mayor, will be cashiered.

MAYOR (*frightened*). Really?

OLMERS. And you, Herr Vice-Churchwarden, will be condemned to prison.

HERR STAAR. Without mercy?

OLMERS. However, I take everything on myself and guarantee a happy outcome.

MAYOR. If you could do it—

HERR STAAR. Brother, keep in mind that your girl is ruined in Piffelheim anyway. In the middle of the night, in the street for all to see, in the company of a young man—no one will have her from now on.

SPERLING. I, at any rate, won't have her.

MAYOR. But even if I agreed--because of the critical aspects—there's still the grandmother—

LOTTE. Olmers has a title.

MAYOR. Are you sure?

FRAU STAAR (*at the window*). Have all the evil spirits broken loose tonight?

---

[20] Continuing from note 6, we can now see that even without a title, Olmers is in a position to win Lotte, for no one doubts that he is a friend of the Minister. The title, however, enables Kotzebue to end his play on a high comic note, and one that is thematically appropriate, as will be apparent when Frau Staar makes her entrance in a few moments.

What witchery is afoot beneath my window?

MAYOR. Just in time. Kindly join us, mother. We're celebrating an engagement.

FRAU STAAR. In the street? Under the open sky? In the dark of the night? Very proper, I'm sure. (*She bangs the window shut*)

MAYOR (*to Olmers*). One thing I must tell you, sir. The affair with our delinquent must be taken care of; otherwise no wedding.

OLMERS. You have my absolute guarantee.

[12] (*Enter Frau Staar in nightdress*)

FRAU STAAR. Well, Herr Assistant Inspector of Buildings, Roads, and Mines, what literary tomfoolery are we up to now?

SPERLING. No, madam. I'm not the person in question here.

MAYOR. Herr Olmers wants to marry Lottchen. And Lottchen wants to marry him.

FRAU STAAR. And *that's* the reason you vexed me out of my bed? It seems to me you heard my decision today loud and clear. The answer is no; out of the question.

HERR STAAR. New considerations have cropped up.

FRAU STAAR. They're nothing to me.

MAYOR. The gentleman can help us out of a great embarrassment.

FRAU STAAR. I don't care.

HERR STAAR. Young miss here carried on with him behind the lamp post.

FRAU STAAR. So much the worse.

MAYOR. She can never find a husband now.

FRAU STAAR. Let her die as a respectable old maid.

MAYOR. The gentleman has money—

FRAU STAAR. Pooh.

HERR STAAR. A fine character—

FRAU STAAR. Pooh, pooh.

MAYOR. And a presentable title.

FRAU STAAR. A title? What sort of title?

OLMERS (*producing his pocket-book*). If Frau Deputy Collector of the Revenue would be so kind as to glance at this document, I flatter myself that Frau Deputy Collector of the Revenue will surely—in light of the elevation of mind for which the Frau Deputy Collector of the Revenue is known throughout the world—

FRAU STAAR (*appeased*). Well, well, the gentleman is a polite gentleman. That much I'm obliged to grant him. What did you say is your title?

OLMERS. Confidential Crown Commissioner.

FRAU STAAR. Commissioner!

HERR STAAR. Crown Commissioner!

MAYOR. Confidential Crown Commissioner!

FRAU STAAR. That, to be sure, alters the situation. Nothing confidential has ever been seen in our family. Under the circumstances, if the Herr Confidential Crown Commissioner would vouchsafe our house the honor—

OLMERS. My happiness rests wholly in the hands of the Frau Deputy Collector of the Revenue.

FRAU STAAR. Herr Confidential Crown Commissioner may count on me.

OLMERS. Frau Deputy Collector of the Revenue is goodness itself.

FRAU STAAR. And Herr Confidential Crown Commissioner is a model of decorum.

MAYOR. That's settled then. Children, come into the house so we can write up the marriage contract and arrest warrant at the same time.

HERR STAAR. Bravo! And let's make a punch. I'll go for the lemons. (*Exits into his house*)

OLMERS. May I aspire to the honor of offering my arm to the Frau Deputy Collector of the Revenue?

FRAU STAAR. Herr Confidential Crown Commissioner will ever find in me his devoted servant.

(*Olmers takes her into the house*)

MAYOR (*to Sperling*). You mustn't blame me, my dear sir. When the fatherland's in trouble a good patriot may have to to sacrifice his daughter to Moloch. (*Exit*)

SPERLING. Your obedient servant!

LOTTE (*to Sperling*). Herr Assistant Inspector of Buildings, Roads, and Mines, I beg the favor of a wedding poem.

(*She exits with a deep curtsy*)

SPERLING. Just you wait. I'll write such a satire—a work of art![21]

KLAUS. I can see that woman sitting behind some hedge feasting on my sausages.

SPERLING. Come upstairs with me, Herr Klaus. I'll let you hear my triplets to our gallows.

KLAUS. Hang your trips. Better find my ham for me. (*Exit*)

SPERLING (*alone*). Is my poem going to go to waste? Now if the night watchman would only come back—(*to the public with dulcet politeness*) or wouldn't one of you care to join me upstairs and listen to my triolets?

CURTAIN

---

[21] This replaces Sperling's "I'll write you an Honor Portal, a work of art!"—another reference to Schlegel's miscellany. Goethe censored all the passages aimed at the Schlegel brothers, replacing them with feeble generalities.

Bibliography

The list below constitutes but a fraction of a hypothetical complete Kotzebue bibliography. Several titles in this list can be consulted for nearer approaches to completeness, namely Goedeke 1893 and 1966, Stock 1971, and Mathes 1972. In particular, I have made no attempt to give a bibliography of editions of Kotzebue's own works. Nor do I list the many English translations of his plays. For these, the Catalogue of the British Museum should be consulted, or else Thompson 1928. On the scholarly and critical side, I regret to say that very little useful material is available in English. I have used the abbreviations K or AvK wherever Kotzebue's name appears in a title. When more than one title is given for an author, the titles are listed in chronological order.

Albertsen, L. L. "Internationaler Zeitfaktor K: Trivialisierung oder sinvolle Entliterarisierung und Entmoralisierung des strebenden Bürgers im Frühliberalismus?" *Sprachkunst* 9 (1978) 220-240.

Anonymous. *Kotzebuana, das ist . . . Merkwürdigkeiten in Leben, Thaten und Schriften des . . . Schauspieldichters AvK*. Hamburg, n. d.

_____. "K heute gesehen." *Literatur: Monatsschrift für Literaturfreunde* 38 (1935/1936) 402-403.

Bailly, M., ed. *La petite ville allemande de AvK*. Paris 1884. [Other printings: 1887, 1891, 1893, 1896].

Behrmann, A. "K on the American Stage." *Arcadia* 4 (1969) 274-284.

Brachvogel, A. E. *Geschichte des Königlichen Theaters zu Berlin*, vol. 2. Berlin, 1878.

Brückner, P. " . . . bewahre uns Gott in Deutschland vor irgendeiner Revolution!" Die Ermordung des Staatsrats von K durch den Studenten Sand*. Berlin, 1975.

Burkhardt, C. A. H. *Das Repertoire des Weimarischen Theaters unter Goethes Leitung 1791-1817*. Hamburg and Leipzig, 1891.

Carlyle, T. "German Playwrights" [1829]. In *Critical and Miscellaneous Essays*, vol. 1. London, 1888.

Charue-Ferrucci, J. "'Krähwinkel' et le vieux Wiener Volkstheater." *Austriaca* 8 (1982) 103-117.

Coleman, A. P. "K and Russia." *Germanic Review* 5 (1930) 323 ff.

_____. "The Siberian Exile of K." *Germanic Review* 6 (1931) 244-255.

Cramer, F. *Leben AvKs*. Leipzig, 1820.

De Boor, H. and R. Newald. *Geschichte der deutschen Literatur*, vol. 6, pt. 1. Munich, 1967.

Denis, A. "La fortune littéraire et théâtrale de K en France." *DAI* 38 (1978) 3125 C.

Döring, H. *AvKs Leben*. Weimar, 1830. [This basic biography also offers a useful chronological survey of K's works, and an indispensable list of sources for a Life of K].

De Vries, J. B. "AvK: His Popularity on the Early American Stage." *Schatzkammer* 2 (1976) 33-42.

Erenz, B. "Dallas 1788: K und seine Erben." *Die Zeit*, 13 December 1985, pp. 49-50.

Erman, H. *Berliner Geschichten, Geschichte Berlins*. Herrenalb, 1966.

Geiger, L. *Berlin 1688-1840: Geschichte des geistigen Lebens der preussischen Hauptstadt*, vol. 2. Berlin, 1895.

Giesemann, G. *K in Russland*. Frankfurt a/M, 1971.

Glatzer, R. *Berliner Leben 1648-1806*. East Berlin, 1956.

Goedeke, K. et al. *Grundriss der deutschen Dichtung aus den Quellen*. Second edition, vol. 5, pt. 2, pp. 270-288. Dresden, 1893. [The basic bibliography, plus critical notice; updated in the Berlin 1966 edition, vol. 15, pp. 151-278].

Gottschall, R. *Die deutsche Nationalliteratur des 19. Jahrhunderts.* Second edition, vol. 1. Berlin, 1861. [This work went through seven editions up to 1901-1902].

Guignard, R., ed. *K: Die deutschen Kleinstädter.* Paris, 1952.

Hertz, D. *Jewish High Society in Old Regime Berlin.* New Haven, Conn., 1988.

Holl, K. *Geschichte des deutschen Lustspiels.* Leipzig, 1923.

Jacob, H. "Ks Werke in Uebersetzungen." In *Studien zur neueren deutschen Literatur*, ed. by H. W. Seiffert, pp. 175-184. Berlin, 1964.

Kahn, R. L. "Personality Factors in K's Work." *Philological Quarterly* 30 (1951) 69-85.

_____. "K's Treatment of Social Problems." *Studies in Philology* 49 (1952) 631-642.

_____. "K's 'Weltanschauung'." *Modern Language Forum* 38 (1953) 41-55.

Kindermann, H. *Theatergeschichte der Goethezeit.* Vienna, 1948.

_____. *Theatergeschichte Europas*, vols. 4 & 5. Salzburg, 1961-1964.

Klingenberg, K.-H. *Iffland und K als Dramatiker.* Weimar, 1962.

Köttelwesch, C. *Bibliographisches Handbuch der deutschen Literaturwissenschaft 1945-1969*, vol. 1. Frankfurt a/M, 1973.

Kotzebue, A. von. *Fragmente über Recensenten-Unfug.* Leipzig, 1797.

_____. *Sketch of the Life and Literary Career of AvK, with the Journal of his Tour to Paris at the Close of the Year 1790.* London, 1800.

_____. *The Most Remarkable Year in the Life of AvK, Containing an Account of his Exile to Siberia.* London, 1802.

_____. *Travels from Berlin, through Switzerland, to Paris, in the Year 1804.* London, 1804.

_____. *Travels through Italy, in the Year 1804 and 1805.* London, 1806.

_____. *Politische Flugblätter* in two volumes. Königsberg, 1814-1815.

_____. *Aus AvKs hinterlassenen Papieren.* Leipzig, 1821.

_____. *Theater* in 40 volumes [index provided]. Leipzig and Vienna, 1840-1841. [Omits *Doctor Bahrdt*].

_____. *Ausgewählte prosaische Schriften* in 45 volumes. Vienna, 1842-1843.

_____. *Doctor Bahrdt mit der eisernen Stirn, oder die deutsche Union gegen Zimmermann.* In *Deutsche Literatur-Pasquille,* edited by F. Blei, vol. 1. Leipzig, 1907.

_____. "Meine verschiedenen Bestimmungen im bürgerlischen Leben," edited by W. Müller. *Jahrbuch der Sammlung Kippenberg* 2 (1922) 171-213.

_____. "Memoire über den Revolutionsgeist," edited by H. J. Schreckenbach. *Weimarer Beiträge* 1957, pp. 86-112. [I have not seen this item].

_____. *Das merkwürdigstes Jahr meines Lebens.* Munich, 1965. [A modern reprint of the 1801 text].

_____. *Vom Adel.* Königstein/Ts 1978. [A modern reprint of the 1792 text].

Kotzebue, C. von. "Mitteilungen aus Ks Nachlass," with notes by A. Leitzmann. *Deutsche Rundschau* 37 (July 1911) 85-102.

Kotzebue, W. von. *AvK: Urtheile der Zeitgenossen und der Gegenwart.* Dresden, 1881.

Krause, M. *Das Trivialdrama der Goethezeit, 1780-1805: Produktion und Rezeption.* Bonn, 1982. [Bibliography lists contemporary reviews of *Die deutschen Kleinstädter*].

Kreisler, E. "K-Briefe." *Euphorion* [Ergäntzungsheft], 8 (1909) 115-119.

Kuhnert, R. *Urbanität auf dem Lande: Badereisen nach Pyrmont im 18. Jahrhundert.* Göttingen, 1982.

Lindsay, D. W. "K in Scotland, 1792-1813." *Publications of the English Goethe Society* 33 (1963) 56-74.

Lombard, E., ed. *La petite ville allemande de AvK*. Paris, 1889. [Reprinted in 1891].

Mann, O. *Geschichte des deutschen Dramas*. Stuttgart, 1963.

Mathes, J. "Aus Briefen Ks an seinem Verleger Kummer." *Jahrbuch des freien deutschen Hochstifts*, 1969, pp. 233-307.

_____. "Ks Briefe an seine Mutter." *Jahrbuch des freien deutchen Hochstifts*, 1970, pp. 304-436. [See also a "Nachtrag" in the *Jahrbuch* for 1971, pp. 483-485].

_____, ed. *Schauspiele* by AvK. Introduction by B. von Wiese. Frankfurt a/M, 1972. [Important bibliography].

Maurer, D. *AvK; Ursachen seines Erfolges: Konstante Elemente der unterhaltenden Dramatik*. Bonn, 1979.

Minor, J. "K als Lustspieldichter." *Bühne und Welt* 12 (1911) 104-114.

Nedden, C. A. zur, ed. *Die deutschen Kleinstädter* by AvK. Stuttgart, 1954.

Picard, L. B. *La petite ville*. In *Oeuvres*, vol. 3. Paris, 1821.

Pütz, P. "Zwei Krähwinkeliaden 1802/1848." In *Die deutsche Komödie*, edited by W. Hinck, pp. 175-194. Düsseldorf, 1977.

Rabany, Ch. *K, sa vie et son temps, ses oeuvres dramatiques*. Paris 1893. [Extremely useful annotated list of Kotzebue's plays, fictions, and periodicals, in chronological order].

Rieck, W. "Doktor Bahrdt mit der eisernen Stirn. Zimmermann und K im Kampf gegen die Aufklärung." *Weimarer Beiträge* 1966, no. 5/6, pp. 909-935.

Schäfer, C. and C. Hartmann. *Die Königlichen Theater in Berlin*. Berlin, 1886.

Schlegel, A. W. *Sämtliche Werke*, vol. 1. Leipzig, 1846.

Schlösser, R. "Schillers Brief an K über die 'Deutschen Kleinstädter'." *Euphorion* 10 (1903) 101-105.

Schneider, F.: "K en España. Apuntes bibliográficos e historicos." *Modern Philology* 25 (1927) 179-194.

Schröder, W.: *Burschenturner im Kampf um Einheit und Freiheit.* East Berlin, 1967.

Schumacher, H., ed.: *Die deutschen Kleinstädter* by AvK. Berlin, 1964.

Sellier, W.: *K in England.* Leipzig, 1901.

Staël, Madame de.: *Germany.* London, 1814.

_____: *Correspondance générale,* ed. by B. W. Jasinski, vol. 5, pt. 1. Paris, 1982.

Steffens, H.: *Ueber Ks Ermordung.* Breslau, 1819.

Steinmetz, H.: *Die Komödie der Aufklärung,* second edition. Stuttgart, 1966.

Stock, F.: *K im literarischen Leben der Goethezeit: Polemik, Kritik, Publikum.* Düsseldorf, 1971. [Important bibliography].

_____.: "AvK." In *Deutsche Dichter des 18.Jahrhunderts,* edited by B. von Wiese, pp. 958-971. Berlin, 1977.

Svoboda, K. J.: "'Kleine Kotzebuana'." *Ruperto-Carola* 21 (1969) 80-84.

Taylor, H. U. Jr.: "The Drama of AvK on the New York and Philadelphia Stages from 1798 to 1805." *West Virginia University Philological Papers* 23 (1977) 47-58.

Thompson, L. F.: *K, a Survey of his Progress in France and England, Preceded by a Consideration of the Critical Attitude to him in Germany.* Paris, 1928.

Varnhagen von Ense, K. A.: *Denkwürdigkeiten des eignen Lebens,* volumes I-III of *Werke,* ed. by K. Feilchenfeldt. Frankfurt a/M, 1987. [Original publication from 1837 to 1859]

Vehse, E.: *Preussische Hofgeschichten,* newly edited by H. Conrad, vol. 4, Munich, 1913.

Wicke, V. G.: *Die Struktur des deutschen Lustspiels der Aufklärung. Versuch einer Typologie.* Bonn, 1965.